Praise for
Learning from Experience

Secretary Shultz's biography, *Learning from Experience*, is full of engaging stories, each of which has a lesson. How he, first of all, "tended his garden" so that when problems arose he was well-positioned to address them: how a diplomat's skill in listening can be more important than his skill in talking; how solutions to knotty problems must benefit both sides if they are to last. But it is more than a retrospective account of an extraordinary life. It looks to the future and offers a visionary guide for success in an emerging new world full of disruptive technologies, shrinking time frames, and uncertainty: "a world awash in change."

*—**William Perry**, a senior fellow at Stanford University's Hoover Institution and director of the Preventive Defense Project at the Freeman Spogli Institute for International Studies, served as US secretary of defense from 1994 to 1997.*

This fascinating book by America's best nonelected public servant of the second half of the twentieth century should be required reading for anyone interested in making public policy. It shows how a thoughtful approach to our national problems by someone who knows what he believes and why changed our world for the better. It shows how important it is for a public official never to stop learning or to fear taking a stand on principle. Again and again you see how head and heart combine to shape results. You also see how candor, preparation, and close observation can generate trust, which is the core of getting something done in our democracy and in the world.

*—**Bill Bradley**, a Rhodes Scholar and American Hall of Fame basketball player, served as US Senator from New Jersey from 1979 to 1997.*

Learning from Experience is a wonderful read. The personal tone and first-hand stories throughout are fascinating, and they are filled with messages and lessons learned in all respects. This book is a very useful contribution to "political-social-economic thought."

*—**John Taylor**, the George P. Shultz Senior Fellow in Economics at the Hoover Institution, served as US undersecretary of the Treasury for international affairs from 2001 to 2005.*

George Shultz's extraordinary and invaluable public service has made our nation stronger, more just, and more secure. George's life—so fully engaged in the toughest of arenas yet so admirably lived—provides a guiding light for citizens and leaders. We should learn from and apply these remarkable lessons as individuals and as a nation.

—*Sam Nunn*, *cochairman and CEO of the Nuclear Threat Initiative, served as US senator from Georgia from 1972 to 1997 and chairperson of the Senate Armed Services Committee from 1987 to 1995.*

The anthology by Shultz of some of his key decisions over decades of statesmanship reflects the author's extraordinary common sense, humanity, and commitment to principle. It should be widely read.

—*Henry Kissinger*, *founder and chairman of Kissinger Associates, served as national security adviser from 1969 to 1975 and US secretary of state from 1973 to 1977.*

learning from
EXPERIENCE

learning from
EXPERIENCE

George P. Shultz

HOOVER INSTITUTION PRESS
Stanford University | Stanford, California

Hoover Institution Press Publication No. 672
Hoover Institution at Leland Stanford Junior University,
Stanford, California 94305-6003

First printing 2016
22 21 20 19 18 17 16   9 8 7 6 5 4 3 2 1

Manufactured in the United States of America

The paper used in this publication meets the minimum requirements of the American National Standard for Information Sciences—Permanence of Paper for Printed Library Materials, ANSI/NISO Z39.48-1992. ∞

Cataloging-in-Publication Data is available from the Library of Congress.
ISBN-13: 978-0-8179-1984-9 (cloth : alk. paper)
ISBN-13: 978-0-8179-1986-3 (epub)
ISBN-13: 978-0-8179-1987-0 (mobi)
ISBN-13: 978-0-8179-1988-7 (PDF)

For Charlotte,

with my thanks for her inspiration and support.

Contents

Contents

PART THREE

PART FOUR

PART FIVE

PART SIX

Contents

Photo Section after page 76

Foreword

Jim Hoagland

THE CONTEMPORARY WORLD is awash in profound and dangerous change, George P. Shultz writes in this groundbreaking book. His extraordinary career as counselor to three presidents and architect to the ending of the Cold War qualifies him to make this sweeping judgment—and to outline the best chances humanity has to avoid disaster at the global level. Most remarkably, he accomplishes this in a conversational, humanistic tone that gives the reader the feeling of sitting by a warm fireside listening to a wise friend describe the lessons that life has taught him at so many levels.

At an early age Shultz, in his own words, "learned how to organize information so as to extract meaning." Here he organizes a lifetime of experiences in government, business, and academia to communicate meaning to a broad audience. I have read many diplomatic histories (and written detailed journalistic analyses for the *Washington Post*) about Shultz's time as Ronald Reagan's secretary of state. But only in reading this account did I come to understand fully how Shultz established the personal trust with Mikhail Gorbachev and other foreign leaders on which state-to-state relations could be built and sustained in a moment of epochal change. It is a talent, and an approach, sorely needed today.

Shultz's prescriptions are notably nonpartisan. William J. Perry, secretary of defense under Bill Clinton, writes in a prepublication comment that *Learning from Experience* shows how Shultz "first of all 'tended his garden' so that when problems arose he was well-positioned to address them; how a diplomat's skill in listening can be more important than his skill in talking; how solutions to knotty problems must benefit both sides if they are to last. But it is more than a retrospective account of an extraordinary life. It looks to the future and offers a visionary guide for success in an emerging new world full of disruptive technologies, shrinking timeframes, and uncertainty."

Shultz's account ranges far beyond the rarefied realm of diplomacy. It illuminates America's race relations, defines a down-to-earth economic philosophy built on free markets and fair treatment of labor, and identifies the strengths and weaknesses of presidential leadership as seen through his time in Washington, including four cabinet posts, in the Eisenhower, Nixon, and Reagan administrations. Looking ahead, Shultz surveys the interrelated technological and political change that has created the need for an updating of the social contract between those who would govern and those who are governed. We may be witnessing, Shultz warns, "the beginning of the end of the modern period and its structure of international relations."

"This book is a very useful contribution to 'political-social-economic' thought," says John B. Taylor, former undersecretary of the treasury for international affairs and professor of economics at Stanford University. "The firsthand stories throughout are fascinating."

In his prepublication assessment, former senator Bill Bradley (D-New Jersey) observes: "This fascinating book by America's best non-elected public servant of the second half of the twentieth century should be required reading for anyone interested in making public policy. It shows a thoughtful approach to our national problems by someone who knows what he believes and who changed our world for the better. It shows how important it is for a public official never to stop learning or to fear taking a stand on principle. Again and again you see how head and heart combine to shape results. You also see how candor, preparation, and close observation can generate trust, which is the core of getting something done in our democracy and in the world."

Shultz brings that experience to bear in examining the hostile forces that today lay siege not only to individual states but to the international state system that the United States helped create out of the ruins of World War II. The acquisition of territory by a movement that has no allegiance to a state but instead is guided by "horizontal" loyalty, dedicated to spreading religious zealotry and destroying national borders, is a particularly dangerous development. The liberal democratic system of politics that was created to ensure that governance could and would promote and protect diversity of thought, belief, and practice is challenged as never before, Shultz writes.

"George Shultz's extraordinary and invaluable public service has made our nation stronger, more just, and more secure," notes former senator Sam Nunn (D-Georgia). "George's life—so fully engaged in the toughest of arenas yet so admirably lived—provides a guiding light for citizens and leaders. We should learn from and apply these remarkable lessons as individuals and as a nation."

And this from Henry A. Kissinger, his fellow former secretary of state: "The anthology by Shultz of some of his key decisions over decades of statesmanship reflects the author's extraordinary common sense, humanity, and commitment to principle."

This book also provides the reader with the keys needed to understand how George Shultz could help bring the nuclear disarmament movement into the mainstream of American policy and politics in the late twentieth century, why he urges his Republican Party colleagues to adopt climate change goals as an insurance policy for this century, and how he shatters other stereotypes, always in a comforting, reasonable manner. As I learned early in getting to know this complex if plainspoken man, you may not know at a given moment what George Shultz is thinking. But you know that he is always thinking, and deeply.

Acknowledgments

I HAVE BEEN BLESSED by the company and the wisdom of many friends and colleagues over the years. They have helped me learn as I've gone along, and I thank them.

In writing about the experiences in this book, I greatly benefited from the help of my editor, Charles Lindsey, and from Charlie Hill, Sid Drell, Alan Meltzer, Kevin Warsh, John Taylor, David Fedor, and Jim Hoagland. My wife, Charlotte, has given me inspiration and ideas, as has my friend Susan Southworth. Judy Leep has typed and retyped the manuscript and has helped pull the book together.

In a few places, I have included material that I treated at greater length in my earlier books, *Turmoil and Triumph: My Years as Secretary of State* and *Issues on My Mind: Strategies for the Future,* as well as in significant articles and speeches. This material is identified where appropriate.

Introduction

SOME YEARS AGO, a man named Alan Bemis told a story at an MIT faculty meeting.

> I'm proud of my appointment as professor, he told the faculty, since it shows that my colleagues and this administration think well of me. But you might be interested in the views of folks in the small town in Maine where I grew up. For instance, two old-timers were listening to the radio and heard the announcement of my appointment.
>
> One said to the other, "I'm not surprised. That Bemis was always a smart kid."
>
> "Yes," came the response, "ever since the first grade, everything that went into his head stayed there, he got to know more and more, and by this time, he knows just about everything."
>
> "That's right," the first one replied. "That Bemis knows everything. But he don't realize nothing."

Bemis was letting his colleagues know that he understood that learning comes in many forms. You learn in your head, but you also learn in your gut and from your experience. And much of the time, especially in a clutch, the learning that guides you comes from experience—from what you *realize*.

This insight was brought home in another way by an assignment President Reagan once gave me as his secretary of state. He wanted me to announce and explain a reasonably important foreign policy decision he had made. I wrote out the speech with great care and took it to the president. He leafed through it, put it down, and said, "Perfect."

There was a dead silence. Then he said, "Of course, if I were doing it, I wouldn't do it this way. You've written this speech to be read. When I give a speech, I speak to the people in front of me or on the other end of a television camera."

He picked up the speech and flipped it open. Then he inserted a caret mark on one line and wrote, "story." He told me, "That is the most important point on this page. If you want to get across an important point to people, you want to get it into their heads but also into their gut, and the way to do that is to tell them an appropriate story. Then they'll realize what you're talking about."

Realizing as well as knowing, learning from experience—these are the broad outlines of how to work your way through the often tense and important decisions that confront us both in daily life and on extraordinary, high-stakes occasions. Putting this book together, I find that I am not trying to write an autobiography but rather, despite a semi-chronological flow, to make a contribution to political-social-economic thought that is unique because of my range of experiences. These are my reflections on how my thinking was formed through those experiences.

I have had the good fortune to be exposed to a great variety of experiences in academia, in the Marine Corps, in cabinet positions, at Bechtel, and, for some twenty-five years now, at a truly exciting place: Stanford University. I have been fortunate to be associated with four of America's great research institutions, where the resources of these creative centers of learning have helped me develop ideas useful in the management of governmental and private organizations.

I have learned how to work with some of the big dichotomies: labor and management, black and white, public and private. I have learned how Washington works and how the corporate world differs from government and teaches different lessons. Through all those experiences runs a realization, sometimes counterintuitive, about how people lead and how people will agree to be led. International order is the broadest field where I have labored and, of course, helping to bring the Cold War to an end was a major part of that. But today we confront in some ways deeper issues as we face the problem of effective governance over diversity in a much more transparent world.

It is my hope that certain lessons about human nature come through. May they be useful in responding to the challenges of a world awash in change—a world fraught with peril and with opportunity.

PART ONE

Durable Lessons

The Market Has an Answer

WHEN I WAS ABOUT TWELVE (in 1932 or so), I decided to start a little newspaper for my neighborhood. I thought I could get it out once a week, so I had the imaginative title of *The Weekly News*. I got up copies, put the price at five cents a copy, and went around to peddle them in my neighborhood. I will always remember knocking on one door and the man of the house, who was a friend of my parents and whom I, of course, knew, looked at what I had to present. He went inside and came back with a copy of *The Saturday Evening Post*, a wonderful magazine with beautiful Norman Rockwell covers. He held it up to me and said, "Here is what I can get for five cents." He declined to buy my newspaper.

My first reaction to this rejection was disappointment, but then I realized that if I were to compete with *The Saturday Evening Post*, I would have to develop some content that was interesting to the neighbors and unavailable to the *Post*. Reflecting on this incident in later years, I realized it was a lesson in the creativity of the market-place. I was led, as if by Adam Smith's invisible hand, to try to come up with something better. Ever since, I have come to expect that in a creative society, market solutions will arise.

I was deeply affected by the Great Depression and the sharp fall in stock values. My father was the creator and the dean of the New York Stock Exchange Institute, so he was a salaried employee and some-what shielded from the ups and downs of the stock market. But every-one felt those large gyrations and struggled to understand them. The talk was all about the market and the money that was being lost, but I remember thinking, even at that young age, that the real problem was unemployment and the lack of productive jobs that gave us the goods and services we needed. I had a sense there was a real economy and a money economy. The two are tightly linked, of course, and one doesn't really exist without the other; nevertheless, from an early age my orientation and my reason for being so interested in economics was a concern about the real economy. This preoccupation influenced choices that had a big impact on my life and, in the policy area, on the views I espoused and the issues I worked on. I became more interested in labor markets than financial markets, even fully recognizing their vital interactions.

Everyone Learns, Including the Leader

I HAVE ALWAYS LOVED SPORTS. My father played football as an undergraduate at DePauw University and he encouraged my interest, which I pursued in high school and at Princeton.

Sports is celebrated as a blend of experience and accountability. Golf is an obvious example: there you are on the green, there's the hole, there's the ball, and you are holding the putter. You hit the ball and the result is unambiguous. Whether or not you sink your shot is solely up to you and the quality of your experience. That accountability factor is unavoidable in all sports, whether individual or team. It becomes natural to extend those insights—to realize the importance of accountability in any system for it to work well.

A good team effort means everyone does his job. If only one member falls down, the team suffers.

At Princeton, I learned something else that affected my style of work in all my later years. During senior year, I showed up for preseason football practice in my best-ever physical condition. I was doing really well until I was blocked across the back of my knees—clipped— and was out for the season. Since I knew the system, I was asked to coach the backfield of the freshman team.

At first I told the squad what to do. Before long, I realized that nothing was getting through: no matter what I "taught," the only thing that mattered was what they learned. I realized that my job as a leader, in this and in many subsequent jobs, was to create a situation in which everyone learned, including me. Then I would have a hot group. What is the problem faced by the offensive backfield? How do we solve it? What are our skills and how do we make the best of them? Once we started asking these questions, the Princeton play system could take its place as an important contribution to solving the problem.

Challenge the Numbers

I STUDIED, TOO. I majored in economics and also was involved in what was then known as the School of Public and International Affairs. It ran a session each semester on a domestic and then an international policy area in which each student was given a role, such as secretary of the treasury or foreign minister of Japan, so we worked at the problem from a position of responsibility. It quickly became clear that having a policy was not enough: you had to pay attention to *execution*. These exercises started me thinking beyond the process of policy formulation to the importance of carrying out whatever it was you decided to do.

I also learned a lot doing a senior thesis at Princeton. My topic was the agricultural program of the new Tennessee Valley Authority (TVA), a plan to distribute fertilizer to farmers in exchange for agricultural practices that conserved the land. During a summer fellowship I went to Washington and collected statistics, and then to the TVA's headquarters in Knoxville for more data, and somehow ended up spending two weeks living with a hillbilly couple on their demonstration farm.

These two interesting people had no education but I could see they were very smart. Interviewing them turned me into a patient listener: the idea was to sit on the porch and rock until they started a conversation. After a while, when they had confidence in me, they asked for my help filling out government forms. They knew what the government wanted to hear and they were determined not to say anything that wasn't true. So the form was filled out honestly. Everything, however, was slanted to what the government wanted to hear.

When I got back to Princeton, it dawned on me that all the numbers I had collected that summer had the same problem. The data from Washington and Knoxville were summations of forms just like the ones I had helped to fill out, so every number had a bias. Ever since, whenever I look at numbers, I ask where they come from. Surveys and polls and questionnaires are inevitably biased and need to be not just tabulated but deciphered.

When I studied for my PhD in economics at the Massachusetts Institute of Technology some years later, I looked into issues involving the job market, such as unemployment compensation and Social Security. I was also interested in union-management relations and the collective bargaining process. Clearly, government intervention in the labor market was sometimes positive, sometimes disruptive. Also clear was the market's ingenuity, especially in economically stressful times.

My PhD thesis was about the men's shoe industry, a competitive business with many producers and lots of market pressures. Not too far from Cambridge, Massachusetts, was the city of Brockton, then a center for the production of high-quality shoes. The statistics I collected on wage rates in Brockton showed very little movement during the deep Depression of the 1930s. I found this puzzling and started thinking in terms of economic theories of sticky wages. When I mentioned this problem to union or management people in Brockton, they mentioned something else: the grade system. The rate of pay, the piece rate, that a worker collected for doing a particular operation was higher for a high-priced shoe than for a cheaper one. Plants could shift from one "grade" to another, not just for production reasons but as a negotiating tactic. Moving to a lower grade could be accompanied by a promise of increased volume, for example. But the stated wage would not change.

This murky series of shoe grades, never fully satisfactory to either labor or management, nonetheless offered a workable way for unions to try to prop up wages and retain jobs, and manufacturers to hold the line on labor costs and stay in business.

Once again I learned to look for things happening behind the ostensible numbers. I was also reminded, not for the last time, that people are usually smarter than you give them credit for.

No Empty Threats (or Reckless Ones)

SOMETIMES SMALL EVENTS have a major impact on your thinking. I remember boot camp and the day my Marine Corps drill sergeant handed me my rifle. "This is your best friend," he said. "Take good care of it and remember: never point this rifle at anybody unless you're willing to pull the trigger." The lesson—no empty threats—was one I have never forgotten. Its relevance to the conduct of diplomacy is obvious, yet often ignored. If you say something is unacceptable but you are unwilling to impose consequences when it happens, your words will lose their meaning and you will lose credibility. But the lesson is also broader, as in any deal-making. If you are known as someone who delivers on promises, then you are trusted and can be dealt with. As my friend Bryce Harlow often said, "Trust is the coin of the realm."

At the same time, we should never lose sight of the consequences of our threats or decisions. One memory of combat sticks with me. During World War II there was a sergeant named Palat in my outfit who was an absolutely wonderful human being. I had tremendous respect and admiration for him. During an action I ran over to where I thought Palat would be and yelled so that I could be heard above the din, "Where the hell is Palat?" After a brief pause came the answer: "Palat's dead, sir." The reality of war hit me hard. Wonderful people get injured and killed.

I often thought about Palat when I was in a position to advise President Reagan on the use of force. Be careful. Be sure the mission is a good one. Be sure your forces are equipped and staffed to win.

The worst day of my life was October 23, 1983, when, as secretary of state, I was awakened to be told that 243 Marines had been killed in a suicide bomb attack on their barracks in Beirut. They were there on a peacekeeping mission. Surely they should have done a better job of laying out a perimeter defense in such a volatile area, but what, I asked myself over and over, should we have done differently? How could we have made their mission a better one?

In the Reagan era, we believed in peace through strength, but we used that strength very sparingly. We used force only three times during the eight years of Ronald Reagan's presidency, and each time its use was sharp but limited. (Reagan, who always realized the importance of executing policy and not just announcing it, started to attract world notice when he fired the striking air-traffic controllers, who had broken their oath of office. He kept the planes flying. It was an early sign that, as many people said, "This guy plays for keeps.")

The first use of force was in Grenada, where some three hundred Americans were virtually held hostage by a murderous Cuban-supported regime that had taken over from the previously democratically elected government. The island democracies in the Caribbean wanted American help in ousting Grenada's regime but our requests to bring out the Americans by ship or plane were denied.

Our use of force was quick and decisive. The Americans were brought home; the first one to land knelt down and kissed the ground. We restored the previous democratically elected government, got Grenada back on its feet, and left. This was in fact the first use of force by the United States since the Vietnam War and it established that, if necessary, we would use our military capability.

The second use of force was retaliation against Libyan leader Muammar Gadhafi for ordering an attack on our soldiers in Berlin in 1986. We knew the building from which the attack orders originated. With a beautifully coordinated operation, the Navy and Air Force took out the building, and the operation was over.

Then, when Iran was interfering with Kuwaiti shipping in the Persian Gulf in 1987–88, we reflagged the tankers as American vessels and put them under the protection of the US Navy. While Iran's president, Ali Khamenei, was making a speech to the United Nations saying the last thing Iran would do was to put mines in the Persian Gulf, we had Navy eyewitnesses taking pictures of Iranian forces doing just that. In one notable operation in September 1987, our sailors boarded an Iranian vessel, seized mines as evidence, removed the crew, and sank the ship. There was no loss of life, but we sent a clear message. We exposed the Iranians' lie, let them know that we knew what they were doing, and showed them the consequences.

But strength and use of force are not the same. President Reagan's buildup of our military power, the vibrant economy he brought about, and his contagious optimism are examples of strength without the use of force. Perhaps our most significant demonstration of strength came in 1983, after the failure of arms control negotiations with the Soviets. In that year, the NATO alliance countries, demonstrating great steadfastness amid an atmosphere of Soviet-generated threats of war, moved ahead in deploying intermediate-range nuclear forces (INF) missiles. I will mention that period again when discussing the end of the Cold War.

Terrorism, and the new responses it would demand, was already on our radar in those days. In October 1984, I spoke about terrorism, labeling it a form of political violence and calling for a coherent strategy to deal with it. My speech [see Appendix] was not welcomed by some but, fortunately for me, Ronald Reagan was in total agreement. We needed a realization in our country about the need to defend ourselves, I said. We had to have "broad public consensus on the moral and strategic necessity of action. . . . We cannot allow ourselves to become the Hamlet of nations, worrying endlessly over whether and how to respond." Clearly, we needed to beef up our intelligence capabilities, I argued, provocatively at the time, and "our responses should go beyond passive defense to consider means of active prevention, pre-emption, and retaliation." But I also warned:

[Terrorists] succeed when governments change their policies out of intimidation. But the terrorist can even be satisfied if a government responds to terror by clamping down on individual rights and freedoms. Governments that overreact, even in self-defense, may only undermine their own legitimacy, as they unwittingly serve the terrorists' goals. The terrorist succeeds if a government responds to violence with repressive, polarizing behavior that alienates the government from the people. . . .

Terrorism is a contagious disease that will inevitably spread if it goes untreated. We need a strategy to cope with terrorism in all of its varied manifestations. We need to summon the necessary resources and determination to fight it and, with international cooperation, eventually stamp it out.

The speech caused considerable controversy, especially my call for preventive action. I considered that to be practically a no-brainer. But then I was closer, as secretary of state, than were many others to acts of terror focused on our embassies and more aware, I thought, of the threat of terrorist acts closer to home. We did beef up our intelligence and a number of acts of terror were prevented because we intervened in time to stop them.

Sometimes the arts of strength are subtle and require not charging ahead but holding back. I recall a time in World War II after my Marine unit had taken a little island in the Pacific. We knew that natives on a nearby island made grass skirts, log canoes, and other souvenirs that we liked to send home. Occasionally, Marines were allowed to go to the island to trade, but for only two hours, so they wanted to make deals quickly. I noticed that the natives enjoyed bargaining. And why wouldn't they? The negotiator who knows you are desperate for a deal will have the advantage. The one who wants a deal too much will almost always have his head handed to him. In this case, we insisted that the locals set a price and stick to it, and then the Marines could decide whether or not to buy.

I kept this realization in mind when President Reagan and I were negotiating with the Soviets. When I was asked at congressional hearings about the importance of making a deal, I would always say we were interested only in *good* deals. Add patience to your strength, and a good deal may come along.

All of these experiences were reinforced by my study of economics. I learned how to organize information to extract meaning, whether or not the information was about the economy. Economics also is about the importance of the lag between an action and its results. So it teaches a truly important lesson: think strategically. Don't be dominated by the tactical issues of the day.

PART TWO

Laboring in the Fields

Everybody Has a Job to Do

BACK HOME after two and a half years as a Marine overseas in World War II, I became a student in the Massachusetts Institute of Technology doctoral program in economics. After receiving my PhD in 1949, I was invited to continue at MIT on the faculty. This was a great compliment and I was honored to accept.

My years teaching at MIT and then at the University of Chicago were times of immense learning. I did a lot of research and wrote books in the general area of labor economics, but I also had the good fortune to be involved in many experiences as a mediator and arbitrator in the labor area. I learned a lot, as well, from spending a year as a senior staff economist on President Eisenhower's Council of Economic Advisers and then in some interesting advisory roles in both the Kennedy and Johnson administrations. All this gave me a storehouse of ideas and useful experiences (my realizations) when I became President Nixon's secretary of labor in 1969.

The MIT Department of Economics was unique: it included in its industrial-relations work some interesting psychologists and a man named Joe Scanlon, who was recruited from his post as research director for the United Steelworkers' Union. Joe had helped a number of steel companies whose costs were out of control and that were threatened with bankruptcy. He rearranged their practices so that the workers had a chance to participate in the way their jobs were set up and managed and, in most cases, get a share of the increased productivity as a bonus, an arrangement that later was called the Scanlon Plan. It resulted in a tremendous improvement in productivity and saved the companies. At MIT, Joe started applying the lessons to profitable companies. I had the privilege of working closely with Joe, and the experience taught me how important it is in any healthy organization that the people you work with have a chance to be involved in what is going on and to make their contribution to, and share in, its success.

As a teacher of MIT engineers, all bright and creative, I felt the need to include in my courses a section on introducing change. Engineers seem to take it for granted that if you invent something new and good, it will automatically take its place. Not so fast! You have to realize that the introduction of change means some things get disrupted. What are they and how are you going to deal with them?

As a case study, I offered the story of William Sims, a Navy officer who eventually rose to the rank of admiral. In the early 1900s, Sims wanted to introduce continuous-aim firing into the US fleet. The system at the time was one in which firing took place at a specific moment during the ship's roll. Sims advocated a system that could keep the guns aimed all the way through the ship's motion so firing could be continuous. He proved his ability to bring this off and argued for what was clearly a more effective use of ships and gunnery. The bureaucracy blasted him. Eventually he wrote to President Theodore Roosevelt, who looked into the new technology and sided with both Sims and his ideas, which also included profound reform of the Navy. The outbreak of World War I showed the value of such disruptive innovation. Sometimes, as my case study showed, it takes a drastic event to convince skeptics.

Challenging the status quo is always hard. Of course, one way to deal with this is to use the power of the competitive marketplace. Someone who resists change will wind up, at the very least, with a lot of unsold inventory.

I also thought a lot about government intervention in major labor disputes. This became almost commonplace in the Kennedy and Johnson administrations, and it resulted in diminishing of the vigor of private negotiations, a symptom of how government intervention changes private behavior. When you know you are going to end up in the White House, you don't make your best offer until you get there.

As I put it to a meeting of lawyers, "If the president hangs out his shingle, he'll get all the business."

On one occasion, I was invited to speak to the Business Council. I included in my speech my reservations about interventions in disputes, including the serious dispute that was then developing in the steel industry. By chance and by surprise, President Johnson was in the audience, but I went ahead with my message. He didn't say a word to me about it, but I had met him earlier and had a very positive experience with him.

I was worried about unemployment in the ghettos and had learned that Johnson was worried about it, too. I was invited to the White House and was asked to be chairman of a small group studying the issue. Johnson made a practice of having little groups—private but not secret—take on subjects of interest to him and make reports to him. I remember him saying to me, "George, if you have a good idea and it turns out to be your idea, it probably won't go very far. But if that idea turns out to be *my* idea, it just might go someplace. Do I make myself clear?"

We did develop a good idea, but, with all due respect to it, President Johnson's execution made all the difference. I experienced firsthand his fabled capacity to get things done. It was another strong illustration of the importance of execution in making good policies work.

Argue About the Problem, not the Principle

IN THE EARLY POSTWAR PERIOD, I had also participated in an investigation into the many strikes marring the labor-relations scene. This effort led to a series of studies of places where peace reigned in the labor-management relationship and problems were resolved. I co-wrote two of the case studies for the series *Causes of Industrial Peace under Collective Bargaining*. This work gave me intense exposure to real-life situations where people learned how to get along.

One of the most durable lessons is that when people are arguing about principles, there is little prospect of getting agreement. The task is to translate the argument into one about the problems. Then, I realized, you have a much better chance of solving them.

I also saw that even good relationships tended to fall apart when people became too concerned about preserving "the relationship." They would push problems aside in the interest of not rocking the boat because they had a good thing going. The relationship then deteriorated anyway—because it wasn't solving the problems of the parties.

I put this realization to good use when I became secretary of state. When I took the post, I noticed that our relationship with China seemed rocky. As I looked into the problems and their causes, I sensed that everything was dominated by the "old China hands," people who had been involved with the original opening to China led by President Nixon and who nourished "the relationship." I had seen this movie before. Concern about the relationship was crowding out concern about substantive issues.

When I first visited China as secretary of state, I said to Deng Xiaoping and my counterpart, Wu Xueqian, "You put on the agenda what you want and I'll do the same. We can then make an agenda out of these desires and work our way through that agenda." The unspoken implication was that the quality of the relationship would be a reflection not of how comfortable we were with each other but of how successful we were at sizing up and tackling problems. The Chinese liked this approach. The Reagan years were a time of good US-China relations.

Seize the Moral High Ground

AT TIMES, problem-solving has to be more confrontational. During my Chicago years I served as co-chairman of the Armour Automation Committee with Clark Kerr, then president of the University of California and a good friend of mine. The meatpacking industry in the 1960s was undergoing a transformation. The large, traditional meatpacking plants to which animals would be driven a long way were being replaced by smaller plants closer to the ranges, thereby having animals arrive for slaughter with more weight as a result of less travel. The Armour Automation Committee was to investigate and report on those momentous changes in the industry, including plant closings and massive layoffs. My experiences working in that field had a major impact on my attitude toward racial discrimination and in thinking through and coming to realize how to deal with that subject.

I knew racial discrimination was a serious problem, but genuine realization arrived only when our team went to Fort Worth, Texas, to see what we could do to help the community and the workers displaced by the shutdown of Armour's plant there.

Our team of four flew to Fort Worth and, before going to the plant, stopped at our hotel to check in. I registered along with my friend Arnie Weber and the clerk said, "Well, we have a nice suite for you." Then the management representative registered and there was no problem.

The union member of our team, who was black, then approached the counter. The clerk looked at him and said, "I'm sorry. We don't have any rooms." The union man pulled out of his pocket something none of the rest of us had: a confirmation slip. So the clerk took it into the back office. He came out and said, "We don't have any rooms."

By this time, my blood was boiling and I said, "You do have a room. You gave me a suite. Put a cot in it and register him." The clerk was so startled that he did it. It turned out that was the first time any black person had been a guest in that hotel.

I realized deep down how irrational and unacceptable these discriminatory practices were. I also saw that when you take the moral high ground, if you speak sharply and with presumed authority, sometimes people do what they should even if they are not authorized to do so.

I had another, more satisfying experience in racial matters in my role as dean of the Graduate School of Business at the University of Chicago. We had a program on campus and another we called a downtown program where people who were working attended school at night. There were a number of black students in our downtown program but none on campus. It wasn't that we were turning people down; the campus program never got any applicants. There's something wrong with that, I thought. So I went around to some of the black colleges and other places where I knew there were large black populations and asked why nobody applied.

I always got the same answers: it's too expensive, and there's no job at the end of that rainbow for us. So I persuaded a few companies with recognized names to put up fellowships and guarantee summer jobs between the first and second years of the program. Recipients didn't have to take the jobs but they were available, and there was no obligation on either side at the end of the MBA program. We managed to recruit some outstanding people, and the program since has been emulated elsewhere.

Racial problems, of course, flared repeatedly in those years and in time I had even deeper experiences with them. Even in the tensest times, though, solutions proved possible if the parties worked at them with determination.

Here is another story from the tumultuous time in the meatpacking industry. Armour had started building a plant in a little town called Worthington, Minnesota, setting into motion a series of events in which I, with others, played a mediating role. As usual, the town was expecting benefits of all kinds; meatpacking jobs were pretty good jobs for those communities. The plant was taking shape when, quite suddenly, the company closed its plant in Kansas City in 1965. It had been there a long while and most of the employees were black. We realized that they had bumping rights—the right of senior workers to displace those less senior—into this new plant. So we went to Worthington, where we found an all-white community. Then we started talking with the town fathers.

The black families started making scouting trips to the town of Worthington to see what it was like. When families came up and looked around, we helped them meet people and get the lay of the land. In those days, there were race riots all over the country, but in this little town, the leaders took a different point of view. They said, "Look, these big cities don't know how to get along with people. We're a little town. We know how to do it. So we're going to try."

One local response was, "Well, we're building this development over here. They can all live there." But the town fathers insisted, "No, we're not going to create a black ghetto. We want them to live around the town." And then when the black families came up, it appeared that many of them tithed to their churches, so the churches started to compete for them.

In the end, quite a few black families moved in, and the transfer worked.

A. H. Raskin, a *New York Times* journalist, went to Worthington and wrote a glowing front-page story on what he observed. In a piece about me, the new secretary of labor, on January 30, 1969, Raskin wrote:

Shultz . . . has served for nearly a decade as co-chairman with Clark Kerr of the pioneering automation committee set up by Armour and its unions in the meatpacking industry. Few companies have had to undergo a more profound adjustment because of new technology, new marketing methods, and new distribution techniques. Packing houses in which workers had toiled for years were closed down, and the workers found the skills in which they had invested a lifetime of application made worthless overnight.

Many of these workers were Negroes and Mexican-Americans, with little formal education and no marketable talents outside a butcher shop. What's more, the bulk of them were well into middle age and employers in their home towns did not roll out the welcome mat when they came knocking on the door for jobs.

In contrast to many other companies confronted with similar shakeouts of personnel, Armour felt it had an obligation to do something positive for its displaced workers. So every time an Armour packing house had to be closed, the Automation Committee was put to work on ways to ease the ax for the employees.

Perhaps the most spectacular of its many successes was in helping Negro workers knocked off the payroll when Armour liquidated its Kansas City packing house. Shultz was in direct command of the re-employment assignment. The chances for finding new jobs in Kansas City proved singularly bleak. Even with retraining, there was little hope for placing the refugees from the slaughter pens and the dressing tables.

The answer Shultz found was to make places for two hundred of them in a new hog slaughterhouse Armour was opening up in Worthington, Minnesota, three hundred miles away. But carrying out that plan was not as easy as it sounds. It is difficult at best to get people with roots in an industrial city to accept the idea of resettling in a tiny hamlet far from any metropolitan center. But what made it all even tougher in this case was that Worthington had never had a single Negro among its ten thousand residents.

Shultz and his associates in the Armour Automation Committee knew it would be suicidal to send Negroes in without any advance effort to assure them of a friendly reception. They did such effective missionary work with the Worthington churches, schools, trades people, and civil leaders that the influx went with incredible smoothness—doubly incredible in the light of the racial tension that grips so much of the country. The experiment is now more than four years old, which puts it safely past the experiment stage.

Even though the task looked difficult, deep consultation and common sense—combined with determination to carry through on a contractual obligation—produced a successful outcome.

Let People Own Their Agreement

OUTSIDE OF PEACEFUL WORTHINGTON, race riots were rocking many American cities. In time, President Nixon made me chairman of a team to manage the desegregation of schools in seven Southern states. It is noteworthy that this happened in 1970, more than a century after the Civil War ended and sixteen years after the Supreme Court, in the case of *Brown v. Board of Education of Topeka,* had declared school segregation unconstitutional.

Even in 1970, schools in seven Southern states were still segregated by law. The *Brown* decision had long since been handed down. Time passed. Tension mounted. The whole subject was intensely divisive, with heated arguments over the problems of busing in areas where the schools were segregated.

In March of that year, the president declared the *Brown v. Board of Education* decision to be "right in both constitutional and human terms" and said he intended to enforce the law. He decided to form a cabinet committee to tackle the problem in a direct, managerial way. Vice President Spiro Agnew was made chairman and I, then secretary of labor, was the vice chairman. (Agnew wanted no part of this effort and essentially declined to participate in the committee's deliberations, so I wound up as de facto chairman.) Our problem was to manage the transition to desegregated schools in the seven affected states: Alabama, Arkansas, Georgia, Louisiana, Mississippi, North Carolina, and South Carolina. Much of the following account, which focuses on how we forged an agreement among parties despite their strong disagreements and antipathy, relies on an earlier book of mine, *Turmoil and Triumph.*

I had strong help in this effort from Presidential Counselor Pat Moynihan, Special Counsel Len Garment, and Ed Morgan, a savvy former advance man for the president. We followed Worthington principles. First, we formed biracial committees in each of the seven states.

We determined, with the president's agreement, that politics should have nothing to do with the selection of the people for these committees. We wanted people, in equal numbers of black and white, who were truly representative of their constituencies. And so, with great care, we selected strong leaders from each of these states.

We didn't pick people who agreed with us or with each other. We chose people who were respected by those they would represent.

The first group invited to Washington came from Mississippi in late spring. We took them into the Roosevelt Room of the White House, directly across from the Oval Office, and started in. The discussion was civil but the deep divisions were evident. The blacks argued that desegregation of the schools would be good for education and that it was absolutely essential. The whites resisted. Both sides were tough but truly representative. We let them argue and get it out of their systems.

Then they got to the point—and this happened with regularity as groups from the other states came in—where I felt that it was time to shift gears.

By arrangement, Attorney General John Mitchell was standing by. He was known throughout the South as the tough guy, and on the whole was regarded by the whites as "their" man. I asked Mitchell what he planned to do as far as the schools were concerned. "I am attorney general, and I will enforce the law," he growled in his gruff, pipe-smoking way. He offered no value judgments and took no part in the debate about whether this was good, bad, or indifferent. "I will enforce the law."

Then he left. No nonsense. Both the blacks and the whites were impressed.

This message from the attorney general changed the playing field. It allowed us to move our discussion forward from "whether" to "how"—to managerial and administrative topics. It was another illustration of how people who dig in their heels over principles can make progress if they convert their argument into one about problems. In fact, desegregation was going to happen. The only questions for these outstanding community leaders were: How would it work? Would there be violence? How would the school system in their community be affected? What would be the effect on their local economies?

They had a great stake in seeing that this effort was managed in a reasonable way, whether they liked it or not.

At lunch, we took the group over to the diplomatic reception rooms in the State Department, where we were surrounded by the artifacts of colonial America, including the desk designed by Jefferson on which he wrote portions of the Declaration of Independence: "dedicated to the proposition that all men are created equal." I sat with the two strong men I wanted to co-chair the Mississippi advisory committee. I had seen their résumés and watched them operate that morning. I argued that if they would accept the leadership, the committee would immediately have great credibility with whites and blacks. Their acceptance would help the committee attain its goal: a desegregated school system with the least possible disruption and the greatest chance to enhance the quality of education for the children.

I saw that I was making headway, so I left them alone for a bit, much to the consternation of an observer from the Justice Department. "I learned long ago that when parties get that close to agreement, it is best to let them complete their agreement by themselves," I told the perplexed observer. "That way, the agreement belongs to them—it's theirs—and they will try extra hard to make it work." As lunch ended, these two tough, respected leaders shook hands on their own deal. We were in business, and in what many regarded as the most problematic state.

Gradually, after we returned to the White House, the whole group came around, and individuals started to make suggestions about how to handle this or that potential problem. A small amount of flexible funds had been set aside, so I was able to reassure the committee members that if they needed money for minor expenditures, I could provide it on a fast track. That seemed to help.

When I felt the time was right, again by prearrangement, I let President Nixon know we were ready for him. We then walked across the hall and into the Oval Office, where he met each of them and sat them down. The president spoke to them with a great sense of conviction and with considerable emotion. Looking around the room, he said, in essence, "Here we are in the Oval Office of the White House. Think of the decisions that have been made here and that have affected the health and the security of our country. But remember, too, that we live in a great democracy where authority and responsibility are shared. Just as decisions are made here in this office, decisions are made throughout the states and communities of our country. You are leaders in those communities, and this is a time when we all have to step up to our responsibilities. I have made my decisions, and I count on you to make yours. Together, we can make this work."

By the time he got through and people were ready to leave, they were charged up. They were willing to get their backs into making the school openings and subsequent operations go forward as smoothly and constructively as possible.

The group that went home to Mississippi was able to provide real leadership. They were all strong people, accepted as legitimate and valid representatives of the true feelings that people within their communities held. We met with delegations from other states before the school year was to start and those meetings went well, too, essentially along the same pattern.

The last state was Louisiana. By then we were confident we could bring about a constructive result—perhaps too confident. I suggested to the president that we hold this meeting in New Orleans—in the South, where the action would take place, not in the lofty atmosphere of the White House. I would do my part in the morning. The president could fly down and do his part with the Louisianans at the end of the morning meeting. Then we would invite the co-chairmen from each of the seven states to join the president and me for an overall discussion of the school openings.

I remember well a meeting in the Oval Office to discuss this possible series of events. Vice President Agnew strongly warned the president not to go. He said, in effect, "There you will be in that room, Mr. President. Half the people there will be black, half will be white. The schools will soon be opening. There will be blood running throughout the streets of the South and, if you go, this will be blood on your hands. This is not your issue. This is the issue of the liberals who have pushed for desegregation. Let them have it. Stay away."

President Nixon looked at me, the nonpolitician in the crowd. I thought he had already decided to go and didn't need arguments from me. But I told him what I thought: "Well, Mr. President, I can't predict what will happen. The vice president may very well be right about violence in the streets, but whatever happens is on your watch. You are the president of all the people, and you and I have seen some very reasonable and strong people come up here. You've met with them and have had a big impact on them. They have been working hard and we have been working with them. We should do everything we can to see that the schools open and operate peacefully and well."

The president decided to go ahead with our plan. Down we all went to New Orleans, except for the vice president, who stayed home.

Pat Moynihan, Len Garment, and I left the night before the president did and started in the morning with the biracial Louisiana group. The going was much tougher than with any other state. As I struggled, I thought the problem might be the nearness of the school opening, the more restricted amount of time, or the missing ambience of the White House. President Nixon was due to arrive about noon to put on his final touch. As noon approached, we had made real progress but had not achieved the degree of agreement I usually secured by the time the president met with the group. We took a recess. I went out to meet with the president. "Mr. President," I told him, "I'm sorry to tell you that I haven't got this group to the point you usually find when you meet with them. This time you're going to have to finish the job yourself."

Nixon came in. He listened. He talked. He raised everyone's sights. He stepped up to the problem, did a wonderful job, and brought them all on board.

That afternoon we had our meeting with the co-chairmen from the seven states, a meeting highly publicized throughout the South. President Nixon talked eloquently about the importance of what was going to happen and the stake that everyone had in seeing it go smoothly. Both whites and blacks made strong pledges of cooperation. A sense of determination in a joint, compelling enterprise filled the room.

As the schools opened, we worried about how the news would be covered on television. Len Garment went around to the leading networks and urged them to report the facts. He said to them, "Suppose a hundred schools open, and there's violence at one of them. What is the story? I think the story is that the schools opened peacefully."

The schools opened, and all went peacefully. The community leaders had done a fine job. They stood up to their responsibilities.

What can we learn from this episode?

First, if you are to give legitimacy to an effort, involve people who truly represent their own constituencies, not people who think the way you do and are easy for you to talk to.

Another major lesson has to do with the development of human relationships among those involved. Deep and abiding hatreds do exist—but personal rapport and respect may still be nurtured. In the desegregation effort we had, in fact, succeeded by using the Worthington principles: deep consultation and common sense.

Most important is leadership from the top. President Nixon stepped up to a tough decision. Then, recognizing the importance of managing the implementation process well, he set the process in motion and took part himself at critical moments.

PART THREE

In the Arena:
The Nixon Cabinet

Competence Counts

BEFORE ACCEPTING A POST in the Nixon cabinet, I had taken time to think about what kind of secretary of labor I might be. I was skeptical of frequent interventions in big labor disputes and I intended to tell the president why. I was deeply concerned about racial discrimination in the workplace. I was a University of Chicago–style free market thinker who would oppose things like an increase in the minimum wage, but I also had lots of experience with organized labor and had established, I hoped, friendly relationships with many union leaders, as I supported the process of collective bargaining.

In the fall of 1968, on leave from the University of Chicago, I was in residence at the Center for Advanced Study in the Behavioral Sciences on the Stanford campus. My family and I were enjoying the beauty and benefits of living in the Bay Area. I had been asked by my friend Arthur Burns to chair a small task force on labor issues with the object of sending recommendations to the president-elect if Richard Nixon were elected. My report was submitted about one day after the election.

Not long afterwards, Burns telephoned me, saying the president wanted to know if I would be willing to accept the post of secretary of labor. I consulted with my family and everyone was enthusiastic. This was a subject I knew well. I also had had experience with the Department of Labor, so I felt well prepared.

I met with Nixon a few days later in Los Angeles, and the president-elect seemed to go along with my views on labor disputes and workplace discrimination. We would face tough policy problems on these issues almost immediately, but one of my initial official actions was merely embarrassing—at least at first.

After the president announced his cabinet in December, I stayed on in Washington and lined up the people who would join me in the other presidential appointment slots in the Department of Labor. The president-elect was pleased and suggested that I bring them all to his post-election office in the Pierre Hotel in New York City. He said, "We'll have a meeting and then you can go down and introduce them to the press and show that my administration is making progress." We had a good meeting with the president and then I took my team to meet the press.

First came Jim Hodgson, nominee for undersecretary. He was a top official at Lockheed. The press asked questions and it was obvious to all: this guy's a real pro; he knows what he's doing. And then, in the back of the room, a reporter raised his hand and said, "Mr. Hodgson, are you a Democrat or a Republican?" Naïve me: it had never occurred to me to ask him. Hodgson said, "I'm a Democrat."

Next up was Arnie Weber. He was dazzling. The same reporter raised his hand: "Are you a Democrat or a Republican?" "I'm a Democrat."

I also had Libby Koontz, a black woman who was soon to be head of the Women's Bureau, and I said, "Well, I'm sure she's a Democrat," which she was.

Finally the press got to Jeff Moore, chosen by Arthur Burns and me to head the Bureau of Labor Statistics. He spoke, and everybody could tell he was a very competent statistician. They asked him his political affiliation and he stood there like a cow chewing his cud. Then he said, "I guess you'd have to say I'm an Independent." I could have killed him!

When I got back to my hotel room, the phone was ringing off the hook. All the Republicans on the Labor Committee were saying, "Don't you know there was an election, and we won?"

I said, "Well, I checked them with the White House and I checked them with the ranking member on the committee." That was Jacob Javits. "Oh, Javits," they scoffed. "He's no Republican!" (though of course he was, but from liberal New York).

When we took office, my team members proved to be very competent. Even some of the skeptics called me to say, "We like your guys." Jim Hodgson became my successor and then ambassador to Japan.

Arnie Weber went on to be the "M" in the new Office of Management and Budget and ended up as president of Northwestern University, where he did a spectacular job. Larry Silberman, my lawyer in the Labor Department, became an important judge in the District of Columbia Circuit.

So I realized that competence matters. Party affiliation is not the only thing that counts, though it could be wise to ask about it.

I realized too that I had lots to learn about politics and dealing with the press and Congress. Fortunately, I had some outstanding mentors.

Tell the Truth, Stand Firm, Follow Through

I PERSUADED Joe Loftus, a premier labor reporter who had worked at the *New York Times* for twenty-five years, to join me as spokesman for the Department of Labor. Joe had seen press spokesmen come and go and he spelled it out for me: "The spokesman has credibility only when reporters know that he is on the inside." He would have to know what was going on, be welcome to attend any meeting, and be well informed. That way, he would never be blindsided. He would conduct himself in accordance with "Loftus's Laws" and he expected me to live by them, too:

- Don't lie. Don't mislead. Credibility is precious; it can never be misused. Once destroyed, it cannot be recaptured.
- Respond to questions directly. Don't be afraid to say, "No comment."
- Never call a news conference unless you have some news. "Why not, even if just for the sake of dialogue and accessibility?" I asked. "Because," Joe said, "reporters make their living by getting their byline in the paper, preferably on the front page. When you call a news conference, they expect a story. Disappointed, they try to create one by goading you into saying something stupid."
- Help reporters get their facts straight. The press is an important way to communicate with the public. Don't act as if reporters are your enemy, however tempting that may be at times.
- Get on top of breaking stories. Be part of the original story because nobody reads the reaction. So be quick and don't hold back. In practice, this means a constant tug-of-war between

the spokesman and officials who are often reluctant or slow to provide needed information.

Ronald Reagan gave me a necktie just as the primaries were getting started in 1980. On it are these words: "Democracy is not a spectator sport." One of the first lessons in Washington is to be a participant. Excellence in government depends on the willingness of talented people to go to work.

But then there is your attitude toward your work. You cannot want the job too much. If you do, you tend to cut and fit, and can all too easily lose your way. You must be willing to stake out a position and stand there when overriding issues of principle are at stake. Public service is not so much a duty as it is a privilege and an opportunity. But public service works only if, in the tensions of these high-pressure jobs, you are true to yourself.

When I started in the Nixon administration in 1969, I was new to Washington and its ways, though I was very familiar with the work of the Labor Department, where I was to be secretary. The press and Congress were mysteries to me. Fortunately, I discovered a man named Bryce Harlow to help me find my way.

Bryce, in my book, was the best congressional strategist ever to hit Washington. I recall going to an instructional session that he chaired. Bryce was diminutive, and he had with him Rogers Morton, a huge man who measured at least six-foot-six.

"I want all you new people to realize how tough it is to deal with the Congress," Bryce said. "Rogers, will you please stand up?"

Rogers Morton stood up, and Bryce, from his height of five-foot-four, said, "Twenty years ago, when I came to Washington, I was as tall as Rogers Morton."

Bryce had a number of simple rules: Return your calls promptly. Deal straight with members of Congress. But he had a complex, intense web of relations with people; sometimes a person was on his side, sometimes not. He was constantly forming and re-forming coalitions to work on a particular subject. People had to know, he felt, that you were a tough adversary and would fight hard and skillfully for your point of view.

"Never agree to do something unless you know that you can do it" was another of his maxims. "If you give your word, then you'd better deliver. That way you develop trust. Trust is the coin of the realm."

Not long thereafter, I put much of Bryce's advice to the test. I started a campaign against racial discrimination in the workplace, having found that discriminatory policies against blacks were rampant in the skilled building trades. In Philadelphia, for example, despite the existence of perfectly capable black workers, there were none to be found in the hiring halls of the skilled construction unions. With strong support from my assistant secretary, Arthur Fletcher, I set out to change this situation by insisting that the unions set an objective for hiring more black workers and create a timetable for attaining that objective.

This effort, which came to be called the Philadelphia Plan, immediately became highly controversial. It took the form of a bill on which hearings were held and a vote taken in the Senate. During those hearings, I was verbally assaulted for trying to establish a quota system. "No," I replied, "I am trying to obliterate one. There has been a quota system in effect for a long time; the number is zero."

Eventually the issue went to the Senate floor. This was my first big Washington battle and I believed that I was on the right side of the issue. After the voting, Senator Hugh Scott of Pennsylvania, the Republican leader in the Senate, gave me his tally sheet. It showed that we had won by a margin of ten: there were 39 ayes (16 Republicans and 23 Democrats) and 29 nays (13 Republicans and 16 Democrats). One of those on my side was Senator Ted Kennedy, a Democrat. In the years to come we became real friends, and he continued to offer valuable support on many issues in the Senate when I was secretary of state.

The Invisible Hand Is Strong

POLITICAL LEADERS want to take charge and show they are getting something done. They know voters often reward action. This urge to intervene, especially in times of crisis, is an important influence on economic policy. Contrast this yearning for political visibility with Adam Smith's famous "invisible hand," which tends to guide the pursuit of self-interest by many individuals toward producing the common good. I have seen many economic situations misjudged at critical moments, often leading high federal officials to feel compelled to intervene. Here are three examples.

When I was sworn in as secretary of labor on January 21, 1969, I inherited a longshoremen's strike on the East and Gulf Coasts. President Johnson had declared the strike a national emergency when it started in the previous October. The Supreme Court, hearing an appeal on the fast-track process provided for under the Taft-Hartley Act, agreed with the president. By the time I took office, the injunction procedures of Taft-Hartley had been exhausted and the strike resumed.

What to do? What to recommend to the president? Since my professorial days, I had been on record as believing that government intervened too much, thereby subverting the process of collective bargaining. I also believed that the possible crises resulting from strikes were vastly overrated. The clear willingness to intervene by officials in the Kennedy and Johnson administrations had led labor and management representatives to exploit this tendency to overestimate the dangers of strikes, duck their own responsibilities, and save their best offers until they got to the White House.

My analysis was that the longshoremen's strike fit this pattern. Yes, it was disruptive to many businesses and employees, but it was not a national emergency. In fact, the disruptions themselves would put strong pressure on the parties to settle their dispute. I told

President Nixon, already preoccupied with the war in Vietnam and disinclined to become enmeshed in a labor dispute, "Your predecessor was wrong, and the Supreme Court was wrong, in judging that this strike will create a national emergency. We should make clear to labor and management that we will not intervene beyond providing mediation services." The president agreed.

We rolled the dice and, after about six weeks, we had made our point. We stuck with that view as the months and years unfolded. As a result, responsibility and accountability returned to unions and management, where it belonged.

I had this experience in mind when I became involved in the battle over whether to bail out the finances of the failing Penn Central Company in June 1970. I had just taken the reins as director of the newly created Office of Management and Budget and the argument was in full swing. A reluctant Deputy Secretary of Defense David Packard was about to authorize, on behalf of the Pentagon, a Defense Department loan guarantee to Penn Central. (The company claimed to provide critical financial and national-defense services.) I found myself arguing with my friend and mentor, Arthur Burns, over whether the financial markets could stand up to what would be a massive bankruptcy. He pushed for what amounted to a bailout. I contended that this would set a bad precedent and that financial markets could hold up under a large bankruptcy. I also wondered what I, a labor economist, was doing disagreeing with the chairman of the Federal Reserve Board on an issue involving financial markets.

I'll never know how President Nixon would have decided the case because at a critical moment his canny political adviser, Bryce Harlow again, provided crucial information and a clear assessment: "Mr. President, the Penn Central, in its infinite wisdom, has just retained your old law firm to represent them in this matter. Under the circumstances, you can't touch this with a ten-foot pole." Suddenly, the expected signing of a guarantee was canceled.

Penn Central Transportation Company filed for Chapter 11, at the time the largest corporate bankruptcy in American history. Burns did a masterful job of maintaining liquidity in the financial marketplace. To my relief, and that of everyone else, no dominoes fell. The management of Penn Central was held accountable for its mistakes and the message delivered to financial markets was a healthy one: no bailouts, even if you are big.

I also noted another important message, as relevant today as it was then: markets are often much stronger than they are perceived to be.

The bankruptcy of Orange County, California, illuminated the idea of accountability somewhat differently. We are familiar with the notion that, if California were a country, its gross product would make it the eighth-largest in the world. Orange County alone has a gross product larger than that of Portugal, Israel, or Singapore.

Risky investments had provided the Orange County government with handsome returns for years. Taxpayers were delighted, but after a time the investments turned sour in a big way—so sour that the county could not meet its immediate financial commitments. Once again the question was posed, this time to California's governor, Pete Wilson: Will you intervene and bail out this unit of government?

Again, a chorus of concern focused on the potentially devastating impact on the system of municipal finance. Governor Wilson stood up to the pressure and Orange County was forced to file for bankruptcy in December 1994.

Municipal finance did not fall apart. On the contrary, the outcome was healthy. Government units all over the country were cautioned to review their investment practices, become more conscious of undue risk (the pension and health care costs had not yet surfaced), and tighten up on supervision: in short, to take responsibility and accountability.

What have I come to realize from these examples? Marketplaces in the United States are strong. They can distinguish good performances from bad, and dominoes will not fall if they are on a firm footing. The free market system is one of accountability, which will work relentlessly against bad performance and reward the good. Intervening in this system of accountability will inevitably change it and can easily result in moving responsibility to the intervener, usually the government and the taxpayers. The players will quickly sense the change and realize that risk profiles have been altered; they can take more presumed risk since they can expect to be bailed out if the risks materialize. Government policymakers must watch out for these presumably unintended consequences.

Of course, I am not arguing that intervention should be ruled out. But individual private companies, no matter how big and interconnected, are not the problem. The problem is how to protect the system, as Arthur Burns did in the aftermath of the Penn Central bankruptcy.

Sometimes It Takes a Crisis

IN 1969 I found myself appointed by the president to chair a cabinet task force on the oil import program. We had a quota system, dating back to when President Eisenhower thought that if we imported more than 20 percent of the oil we used we were asking for trouble in national security terms. By 1969, we were bumping up against that 20 percent ceiling. The job of the task force was to figure out what to do. I assembled a talented staff, and within a week we knew more about this subject than anyone else in the federal government. One of our recommendations was that since oil is a strategic resource, there ought to be some government entity keeping track. We also realized that the security problem wasn't really a military problem but rather a threat posed by the tension between the Israelis and the Arabs. Things could go wrong and suddenly, we warned, you could lose that oil from the Middle East. That was the real threat. So we argued that we should limit our imports from that area and develop a strategic reserve as a little insurance policy. We also recommended that a tariff system should replace the quota, and then the US government would collect the rents created by the system.

All of these recommendations seemed obvious to us. The report was published, the president thanked us, and Congress held hearings, but nothing was done. I began to understand how hard it is to get anything done when all you have is a strategic analysis, however sound.

Four years later, I was secretary of the treasury when we experienced the Arab oil embargo. We had resupplied the Israelis in the 1973 war and this was the Arab countries' retaliation. It was traumatic, of course. A lot of electricity was generated by oil in those days. Christmas lights were frowned upon and in some places prohibited. Gas prices rose and stations closed on weekends. The oil embargo became a national security problem and threw our economy into turmoil. And at that point we basically put into effect our task force recommendations.

So I learned another lesson. When the moment comes and an opportunity is there, you can accomplish something if you are ready. Too often, when opportunity comes, you're not ready—and nothing happens.

The 1973 oil boycott is relevant in another way. As the crisis unfolded, people came to me with ideas about energy efficiency and alternative sources of energy. The ideas were interesting but still in the early stages. I encouraged them. Then, when the price of oil went back down, interest in those potential changes simply dried up. By now we have been riding this energy roller coaster for decades, but I hope the time has finally arrived when we will realize it is time to get off. I will continue working to build support for energy research and development, regardless of whether gas prices rise or fall.

A Word from the Pope

DURING THE OIL CRISIS I kept my eyes open for solutions. Meanwhile the price of oil shot way up and rearranged finances around the globe. World finance ministers agreed to meet in January 1974 in Rome. My late wife, O'Bie, was a devout Irish Catholic girl, and somehow we managed, through White House connections, to arrange a private audience there with Pope Paul VI.

We went to the Vatican and were placed in a little holding room. A monsignor came in, looked at me rather severely, and said, "When the Holy Father is ready, you will come in for ten minutes." Then he looked at my wife and said, "Then you will come in for two minutes, during which time there will be pictures." Then he left. My wife and I looked at each other, thinking, if that's the deal, that's the deal.

A little while later, out came an American cardinal full of good will: "Come on in. The Holy Father is ready." My wife hesitated. "Come on in, come on in," he said. So we both went in and started a very animated conversation with the pope about oil prices and their implications. I was really struck by how much the pope knew about the subject. His positions were very consistent with those of the US delegation.

Our animated conversation went on and on: fifteen minutes, a half hour, then three-quarters of an hour went by. I thought to myself, "Well, maybe it's up to me to bring this to an end, and I should do it on a humorous note." So I said to him, "Your Holiness, the finance ministers of the world have been here for two full days and nothing we've been able to think of has done as much good for this problem as the mild weather we've been having this winter. We thank you for your intervention."

The pope didn't laugh. He looked at me and said, "Mr. Secretary, you may be sure it will continue." We had another mild winter the following year.

Steer by Your Compass

THE OFFICE OF MANAGEMENT AND BUDGET was created in June 1970 and I became its first director. Throughout the early 1970s, I worried about the growing atmosphere favoring wage and price controls. We had the budget under control and the Federal Reserve Board had a sensible monetary policy in place. Unemployment was too high and prices were rising too fast, but the rates of change in both were coming down. Long-run thinking suggested that we should stick with these policies.

I set out to convince people that the proper course was "steady as you go," an approach I advocated in a speech in April 1971:

> The basic strategy of economic policy and its current tactical implementation are generally on course and economic policy can benefit from application of the old nautical phrase, "Steady as you go." . . .
>
> A portion of the battle against inflation is now over; time and the guts to take the time, not additional medicine, are required for the sickness to disappear. We should now follow a noninflationary path back to full employment. . . .
>
> Those of you familiar with sailing know what a telltale is—a strip of cloth tied to a mast to show which way the wind is blowing.
>
> A captain has the choice of steering his ship by the telltale—following the prevailing winds—or . . . by the compass.
>
> In a democracy, you must keep your eye on the telltale, but you must set your course by the compass. That is exactly what the president of the United States is doing. The voice from the bridge says, "Steady as you go."

Unfortunately for the economy, the voice from the bridge decided to say something else. I lost that battle. When President Nixon imposed wage and price controls, the move proved wildly popular at first. But in the end it produced a massive infusion of government regulation accompanied by the dire consequences that many economists, including me, had predicted, including the very inflation the controls were intended to target.

The president had ignored the recommendation to "think long" and the country paid the price in the form of a poor economy in the 1970s. Not until Ronald Reagan took office in 1981 did the United States get back on a sustainable economic track.

You Can't Want the Job Too Much

BY THE TIME I became treasury secretary in June 1972, the international exchange system was in disarray and there was no US plan to restore stability. I set out to create a plan that we could propose at the annual meeting of the World Bank and the International Monetary Fund, always attended by the world's top finance ministers and bankers. I was convinced that the United States and the world would be better off if the exchange rate system were more flexible. But I knew that many throughout the world, particularly in Europe, preferred a system in which exchange rates were more fixed, with par values for various currencies set and not expected to change, unless very gradually. So, out of a conversation I had with Milton Friedman, the idea emerged of a floating exchange rate system with the appearance of par values. All countries had reserves and, under the system we devised, major changes in reserves would automatically create changes in exchange rates.

I spent the summer of 1972 working through the idea of a disguised floating exchange rate system with my government colleagues. My under secretary, Paul Volcker, pulled the laboring oar with great skill and wrote a series of memoranda supporting our plan.

On the Sunday before the Bank-Fund meeting began, I took the unprecedented step of inviting the finance ministers of the major countries to meet with me individually, review the speech I would deliver at the meeting, and offer suggestions. This process was the start of long-lasting friendships with Valéry Giscard d'Estaing of France, Helmut Schmidt of Germany, Tony Barber of the United Kingdom, and, eventually, Takeo Fukuda of Japan. None of them requested substantive changes to the basic US plan, but each offered valuable suggestions that probably contributed to its widespread reception.

With that, the world heaved a sigh of relief, not because every country agreed with the US plan but because the United States was now back in the game with sensible ideas. Eventually, through a series of larger meetings involving some twenty countries and extensive private discussions among the finance ministers in our little group, the world found its way to the present system of loosely managed floating exchange rates.

Problems have cropped up along the way, as right now. The gigantic liquidity created by key central banks has disrupted the system. But the system has worked reasonably well over the years, remaining fundamentally consistent with the recognition by the post–World War II statesmen that competitive devaluations of currencies, like protectionism in trade agreements, are a bad idea.

This experience stood me in good stead later when I was President Reagan's secretary of state because I could reflect on how international agreements might best be forged. It also gave me the chance to develop genuine personal friendships with leaders of other major countries. It was an exercise in seeing not only what could be done but also how to make it happen.

I have remarked on how courageous President Nixon was on many occasions, but he also had a dark side. Here is a story involving the IRS. Johnnie Walters, the IRS commissioner, and I had worked together on a number of issues, particularly our joint struggle to figure out how we might simplify the tax code. One day, he came to me and said, "The president's counsel, John Dean, just came over and gave me this list of around fifty names and said the president wants a full-field investigation of them." (That's a very unpleasant process.) "What should I do?"

I said, "Well, don't do it."

He said, "What will I tell John Dean if he asks?"

I said, "Tell him you report to me, and if he has any problem, his problem is with me, not you." That was the end of the matter. (The Nixon tapes revealed President Nixon saying to John Dean, "Who does Mr. Blue Eyes think he is, not doing what we want him to do?")

When I took over the Treasury Department, I found that the wage and price control system, then in effect for over a year, was in my direct line of responsibility. In collaboration with the two men in charge, Don Rumsfeld and Dick Cheney, I began the process of dismantling the controls. Against my strong advice, President Nixon decided to reimpose them in full.

I have always felt that the jobs I held in government were a privilege and a responsibility, but as I have mentioned before, I also know that you cannot want the job too much or you may do things you later regret. So, when the president reinstalled wage and price controls, I resigned.

"For the first two minutes, I could swear I was dancing with Fred. My warmest regards, Ginger."
1983

I swing for the fences, 1935.

Strategizing with President Nixon.

In the Palau Islands
after the battle, ca. 1944.

Walking with
General Secretary Gorbachev, 1990.

Receiving a prize from
Senator Ted Kennedy,
January 18, 1989.

To Secretary Shultz. A tiger who burned bright in the eyes of Congress and the World. With respect. Ted Kennedy, Jan 89

In my Treasury office—shaking hands with Alexander Hamilton.

Making a point with President Reagan.

Painting the town red, 2008.

A new Secretary of Labor being pushed down the hill by my children and O'Bie, 1968.

I get support from Boris Becker, April 7, 1986.

Our foursome: Lee Trevino, Ronald Reagan, me, Tom Watkins and our host, Walter Annenberg, December 31, 1988.

Warning to any Middle East
negotiator, 1988.

Having a laugh with President Reagan, 1988.

With Foreign Minister Peres and Prime Minister Shamir before my dedicatory remarks at outdoor Yad Vashem, May 10, 1985.

My dedicatory address,
May 10, 1985.

Charlotte and I with four great-grandchildren—our inspiration, 2013.

You're never too old for a hole in one, 2009.

At Camp David with Arthur Burns, John Connally, the President, and Paul McCracken, 1971.

The Seoul
Peace Prize,
1992.

Ready to pilot the
F-15 Eagle, Nellis
Air Force Base, 1985.

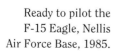

Meeting Deng Xiaoping in Beijing, 1983.

Shevardnadze and I sign a treaty witnessed by Presidents Reagan and Gorbachev.

President Reagan toasts Margaret Thatcher, 1988.

With my friend
Lee Kuan Yew.

Ready for a night
out on the town, 2012.

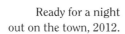

PART FOUR

Schooled in Business
at Bechtel

Schooled in Business at Bechtel

WHEN MY RESIGNATION from the Treasury Department became known, I was offered a lot of chairs at good universities, including Stanford. I said to the dean, "I've been working hard. I don't want a chair, I want a couch." No couches were available.

But I also reflected, "I've had an academic career: I've taught, written books, been a dean. Now I've had a government career. Why don't I try business?" I was surprised and flattered at the good jobs that soon came my way, but the most appealing one came from Steve Bechtel to join his engineering and construction company, based in San Francisco. This was a popular choice with my family because our brief sojourn in Palo Alto when I was at the Center for Advanced Study had given us a taste of the beauty and variety and stimulating environment of the Bay Area. I also liked the idea of being part of a company focused on building projects.

I remember saying to Steve, "I'm joining up, but I don't know much about business." I also wanted Steve to know that I would not be willing to use the contacts I had developed in government on behalf of Bechtel, or anyone else.

But Steve said right away, "George, let's be clear. I don't want you ever to use your friendships with people in government to lobby on Bechtel's behalf. We get by on our merits." Steve's deep integrity, I later learned, permeated the whole organization.

"You know more than you think," he went on. "You know about labor negotiations and you know something about finance, and I'll teach you about construction."

He did this in a clever way. I was made a member of the Bechtel executive committee, whose members each sponsored one or more areas of work. Among my assignments was the Mining and Metals Division, a tough bunch of guys who were proud to go anywhere the minerals were and get a plant going.

The head man was a gifted engineer and a great human being named Bob Cheatham. He told me, "We're glad to have you as our sponsor. You seem to be a pretty good guy and Steve seems to like you, but we know you don't know anything about this field. So if you're willing, we'll teach you." He gave me material to read and we had classes. I noticed he would include others from the mining and metals group, so he was teaching them, too. We also traveled together extensively, calling on clients and visiting completed jobs, partly completed jobs, and jobs that were just starting.

By the time the course was over, I had gained a reasonable understanding of the mining and metals business. The division hosted a big luncheon and gave me a diploma. It's the best diploma I ever received because it meant "We accept you; you're one of us."

I also learned a few things at Bechtel that had broader implications.

Steve Bechtel was a master of delegating authority. Delegation was not abdication on his part. The lines of authority remained clear and the ways of evaluating how the authority was exercised were also clear, so accountability was embedded in delegation. You were also admonished to have "no surprises." If anything unusually bad or good happened, Steve wanted to know about it right away. This is how a skillful leader stays in control without having to constantly monitor all the details.

There were subtler things to be learned through the preoccupation with safety I saw at any Bechtel jobsite. It gradually dawned on me that there are at least two classes of problems, and that you benefit from understanding which is which. Some problems can be solved, but others can only be worked at. Safety, for example: if you put up guardrails and think you've solved the problem, you've lost, because safety is all about attitudes. If you want a world free of accidents—no lost-time accidents—you must work at it every day persistently, creatively, and professionally . . . and if you do this, you just might wind up with millions of accident-free hours not because of some simple, one-time fix but because you realize that the problem is not solvable except through continual effort.

Lots of problems are like this. Understanding the nature of a problem can go a long way toward managing it. For the kind of problems—like safety—that are always a work in progress, I came to advocate during my years in diplomacy a form of "gardening." That is, keep in touch with people so you cultivate the trust that will lead to constructive action.

Steve was also an excellent teacher on the importance of developing leaders. He spent what I regarded as an impressive amount of time identifying promising young people and then figuring out the training and experience they needed to develop their capabilities. Promotion from within was based on an intense effort to develop leadership. It's one thing to look good when things are going well, Steve would say, but how does a guy deal with things when they're falling apart? That's the test.

I put Steve's approach to work in the State Department, as I knew one of my responsibilities was to help develop leaders in the foreign service, our country's invaluable corps of professionals in diplomacy.

PART FIVE

Back in the Arena: The Reagan Years

Accept the Short-Term Cost

IN JUNE 1982 I was attending an important meeting in London as president of Bechtel. In the middle of the meeting, I received a call from Bill Clark, chief of staff of the National Security Council. He asked that I go over to our embassy that afternoon to take a call on a secure phone from President Reagan. I had no idea what the call was about, but after consulting with my wife, who was also in London, we agreed that I should probably do whatever the president wanted if it was within my capabilities.

Over the phone, the president told me that Al Haig had resigned as secretary of state, that the resignation had been accepted, and that he wanted me to accept the job. We knew each other well, having worked together on economic issues as far back as the primaries before he was nominated. After some discussion, I accepted, and by the next morning, my wife and I were on a flight to Washington. After my confirmation in July, I quickly became immersed in foreign policy.

My first extensive contact with Ronald Reagan had come years earlier, when he was governor of California. He invited me to Sacramento after I returned from my three cabinet jobs during the Nixon presidency. There he subjected me to two and a half hours of questioning about how the federal government worked. Clearly he was eager to accomplish something. I could see that while he wanted to be president, he also wanted to execute.

I was chairman of his economic advisory panels during the primaries, the campaign, and the first year and a half of the Reagan presidency. When Reagan took office, inflation was in the teens, and he knew—we all knew—it would have to be brought under control if we were to have a strong, healthy economy.

Paul Volcker was now Fed chairman. I knew him well and respected him greatly; he had been my under secretary when I was treasury secretary. He was doing what we all knew needed to be done, but the political side of the White House kept running into the Oval Office with the refrain, "He's going to cause a recession. We're going to lose seats during the midterm election."

President Reagan would nod. He understood full well the implication of Volcker's policy, but he held a political umbrella over Volcker so he could do what needed to be done.

By the end of 1982, inflation was under control and everyone could see it was going to stay that way. The economy took off like a bird. Reagan had been part of a needed strategic view that took a short-term hit to gain long-term health in the American economy. I have always felt this was his finest hour in domestic policy, and it contributes to my high estimation of the way he understood the presidency.

Unstable Systems Crumble

WE HAD MANY PREOCCUPATIONS when I was secretary of state: developing constructive relationships with the Chinese and with our friends and allies in Southeast Asia, nourishing our NATO alliances, and, of prime importance, paying attention to our neighborhood. We had a vision of North America that resulted in a free-trade agreement with Canada and saw Mexico move in a direction more attuned to the economics of North America.

We knew economics would play a big part in any effective foreign policy. In the State Department we tried to analyze events through an economic lens and figure out ways to strengthen developments that were in our interest. We had a bureau that focused on economic issues, and the analysts there became experts on subjects such as tariffs, fishing rights, quotas, and the like. They were bright, knowledgeable people and creative thinkers but I wanted to inject the analytical capacity of professional economists. I established within State a miniature version of the president's Council of Economic Advisers, made up of professional economists recruited with the help of the president's group. Their job was to put economic reasoning to work on the issues before us.

For instance, as we watched changes unfold in the Soviet Union, I also noted that, with the price of oil staying low, soon the Soviets would be running short of foreign exchange. The USSR depended heavily on international oil sales. The increasing shortfall explained why, when President Reagan once asked Mikhail Gorbachev why he wasn't buying more grain, the Soviet leader replied, "We don't have any money."

So economics was always a strong underpinning of our foreign policy. Of course, the dominant foreign policy preoccupation of the Reagan years was the Cold War.

The Cold War is over. But when did it end and how? The answers are highlighted in battles that took place in Washington in the 1980s, particularly the latter part of that decade. My own role was heavily influenced by what I had learned and what I realized as a result of earlier experiences.

On one side were people, including President Reagan, British Prime Minister Margaret Thatcher, and me, as Reagan's secretary of state. We thought the Soviet system was unstable and, in the long run, would wind up changing. My own views were heavily influenced by what I realized about the weaknesses in the Soviet Union based on my dealings with their leaders while I was secretary of the treasury in the early 1970s.

We were looking for real indicators of change, such as a willingness to draw down nuclear and conventional forces on some mutually agreed basis, as well as a changed attitude toward the Soviet people, including their right to move around internally and to emigrate. The emigration issue was particularly important for Soviet Jews. There was also a realization, on our part, that somehow the Soviet economy was not working anywhere near the potential implied by the talents of its people and the unparalleled natural resources at its disposal. We also recognized that the political system needed to be opened up.

On the other side were people who believed that the Soviet Union would not change, that Mikhail Gorbachev was an aberration, that his reforms were illusory, and that the situation would soon revert to the earlier Brezhnev model. The CIA seemed gripped by this view.

It always seemed to me that Gorbachev was a genuine realist. He was the first Soviet leader to have actually lived in the Soviet system. Previous leaders had all lived in a cocoon. Their wives shopped at special stores and they really had no direct experience with Soviet life as lived by the general public. Gorbachev and Eduard Shevardnadze, minister of foreign affairs, on the other hand, grew up in the system.

They had fought their way to the top and they remembered what life was like at the bottom. I am sure that Gorbachev's trip to Canada in 1983 also had a considerable impact on him: he saw, with his own eyes, a different world.

The clash of ideas went on alongside different assessments of what was actually taking place. Another way to state these differences is to distinguish the policy of détente and the related policy of linkage from the view of those who were opposed to that approach.

The underlying assumption of détente was: We're here, they're there; that's life. The name of the game is peaceful coexistence. With both sides armed to the teeth with nuclear weapons, peaceful coexistence was certainly desirable. Linkage meant that the nature of the peace and the relationship were somewhat governed by events: bad things in one area, such as egregious human rights abuses, would cause disruptions in all other areas.

The most outstanding example of this approach was the reaction of President Jimmy Carter to the Soviet invasion of Afghanistan in 1979. He was shocked and dismayed, and he terminated all contact with the Soviet Union. Our athletes were not permitted to go to the 1980 Moscow Olympics, an arms control treaty was withdrawn from consideration by the Senate, and the annual visit by Foreign Minister Andrei Gromyko to Washington at the time of the UN General Assembly was canceled.

The opposite view was represented by Reagan's emerging attacks on détente in the 1980s. He challenged President Ford's position on détente in the Republican primaries of 1976, saying that Ford was too soft on the Soviets. But as the 1980s unfolded, Reagan's differences with détente came to settle on the view that the Soviet system would change. As he said in a highly publicized speech before the British Parliament in June 1982:

> It is the Soviet Union that runs against the tide of history by denying human freedom and human dignity to its citizens. It also is in

deep economic difficulty. The rate of growth in the national product has been steadily declining since the fifties and is less than half of what it was then. . . .

Overcentralized, with little or no incentives, year after year the Soviet system pours its best resource into the making of instruments of destruction. The constant shrinkage of economic growth combined with the growth of military production is putting a heavy strain on the Soviet people. What we see here is a political structure that no longer corresponds to its economic base, a society where productive forces are hampered by political ones.

The decay of the Soviet experiment should come as no surprise to us. Wherever the comparisons have been made between free and closed societies—West Germany and East Germany, Austria and Czechoslovakia, Malaysia and Vietnam—it is the democratic countries that are prosperous and responsive to the needs of their people. And one of the simple but overwhelming facts of our time is this: of all the millions of refugees we've seen in the modern world, their flight is always away from, not toward the communist world. Today on the NATO line, our military forces face east to prevent a possible invasion. On the other side of the line, the Soviet forces also face east to prevent their people from leaving.

It should be noted that George F. Kennan, the diplomat who originated the idea of containment, held that if the Soviet Union could be contained long enough, its internal problems would eventually cause it to change.

Respect Your Adversaries

MY OWN VIEW about the Soviet Union's future was shaped by my experiences in the early 1970s, when I was secretary of the treasury. One of my jobs was to manage our economic relationship with the Soviets. In the process, I had met periodically with the Soviet team, visiting Moscow a number of times. During any visit to Moscow you could see the streets were practically empty of civilian cars, with movement on the streets more or less limited to the ZiL limousines of the Soviet elite going in and out of the Kremlin. Stores and restaurants showed a clear lack of ordinary activity and the scene was dour.

My late wife, O'Bie, always accompanied me on my trips. She had been a nurse and she frequently would visit a hospital or other medical facility in Moscow. She came back from these visits horrified at the lack of basic sanitation and proper procedures considered routine in any US hospital. I realized their health care system was deeply flawed.

At one point, President Nixon agreed that the Soviets could buy wheat and other grains in the US market. Teddy Gleason, the head of the longshoremen in New York, said, "The president can decide whatever he wants, but I ain't loadin' no grain for no commies." I went down to New York with a colleague who knew Teddy and we persuaded Teddy to load the grain.

The Soviets then quietly bought a little grain here and a little grain there, and by the time the market woke up, they had made large purchases of an immense proportion of available US supplies. Prices in the United States skyrocketed. On a trip to Moscow shortly after that, I met with Alexei Kosygin, the number two man to Soviet leader Leonid Brezhnev. Kosygin was in charge of economic matters. I described what had happened and he acknowledged it. "We can't tolerate this," I said, and he understood.

Out of that meeting came the concept that turned into a long-term grain agreement. It provided for negotiation at the start of each season, leading to an agreement about the amount of grain the Soviets would buy. This was announced publicly so the monopsony power was taken away. I realized you could talk sense to Soviet leaders and make a sensible deal.

Meanwhile, I wanted to know what was happening to Soviet crops. With the president's support, the CIA set out to make estimates. Their satellite photography revealed the areas planted and what went on during the growing season, and before long we had better estimates than the Soviets did. In the process, we learned about Soviet agriculture and our experts were appalled at the low yields from their plantings and from collective farming, the dominant model. It didn't work—yet another clue to the profound weakness of the Soviet system.

At the same time I sensed the Soviets' deep desire for respect, especially related to their role in defeating Hitler in World War II. My opposite number was a crusty old communist named Nikolai Patolichev. We developed a reasonable friendship and he told me some of his life story. He insisted after one visit to Moscow in 1973 that we go to Leningrad. He asked what I wanted to see there. I said I wanted to see the same things that everyone wants to see in Leningrad: the Hermitage, the Summer Palace, and so on. He said, "No, the first thing we will do is visit the cemetery," so we did.

We walked out to a platform from which we could see rows and rows of mass graves. As we walked down between them to lay a wreath at the end of the cemetery, funereal music was playing and Patolichev was telling me about the Battle of Leningrad, which included one of the longest, most harrowing sieges in human history. He was weeping. Suddenly the able woman who was interpreting for us dropped back. I glanced over and she was sobbing, too. Every family in the Soviet Union was touched by the Battle of Leningrad, Patolichev told me.

When we returned to the platform, I said to him, "I have a great sense of community with the people here. I also fought in World War II. I also had comrades shot down beside me. Also, these are the people who stopped Hitler." Then I walked to the front of the platform, stood at attention like a Marine, and gave a long salute. When I came back, Patolichev said, "Thank you, George. That shows respect."

Word got around about this visit. It was an important insight in dealing with the Soviets: don't be afraid to show respect when respect is deserved. It will add credibility to your views, even the critical ones.

My encounters during the Nixon years with Leonid Brezhnev, Alexei Kosygin, Nikolai Patolichev, Andrei Gromyko, and other Soviet leaders, along with my visits to Moscow, would give me a baseline that no one else in the Reagan entourage had.

When I arrived as secretary of state in July 1982, the frozen situation bequeathed by President Carter was still in place and President Reagan's reputation was that of a hard-hitting anti-communist. My friend Helmut Schmidt, chancellor of West Germany, counseled me: "George, the situation is dangerous. There is no human contact."

I managed to get permission for weekly meetings with the Soviet ambassador, Anatoly Dobrynin. The idea was to get rid of little irritants so they would not grow into unnecessarily major problems. These meetings played a chance role in exposing me to Reagan's personal instincts on how we should behave.

Don't Rush to Take Credit

THIS STORY about the importance of trust begins with a snowstorm that unexpectedly kept President Reagan and the First Lady in Washington. Sometimes chance sets key events in motion.

I had just returned from China after a good set of meetings with Deng Xiaoping and my counterpart, Wu Xueqian. I was lucky to land at Andrews Air Force Base because it was snowing heavily. It snowed all day and the next as well, so the Reagans were stuck in the White House. Our phone rang and Nancy said, "How about coming over for supper?" So O'Bie and I went over.

Before long, the president and Nancy started to ask me about the Chinese leaders. "What are they like?" "Do they have a sense of humor?" "Can you find their bottom line?" They knew that as secretary of the treasury I had dealt with the Soviets and a lot of those officials were still in power, so the conversation shifted to the Soviet Union. It dawned on me that President Reagan had never had a real conversation with a big-time communist leader, and he was dying to have one.

So I said to him, "Ambassador Dobrynin is coming to one of my sessions on Tuesday afternoon at five. What if I bring him over here and you talk to him?" He said that would be a great idea, adding, "It won't take very long, because all I want to do is tell him that if his new leader, Andropov [who had just succeeded Brezhnev], is interested in a constructive conversation, I'm ready. It won't take me ten minutes." (Until then, his interest in a meeting with the top Soviet leader had been completely unknown.)

That Tuesday I quietly brought Dobrynin over and we met in the family quarters for at least an hour and a half. We talked about everything under the sun. About a third of the time was spent on Soviet Jews and their mistreatment. The president also came down hard on the issue of the Pentecostals—in the Carter years a number of Pentecostal Christians had rushed into the US embassy in Moscow to publicize the

Soviets' refusal to let them emigrate. Their sect was being persecuted and they were afraid for their lives if they left the embassy. President Reagan kept saying to Dobrynin, "It looks like a big neon sign you've got up in Moscow saying that you don't treat people right, you don't let them emigrate, and you don't let them worship the way they want. You ought to do something about it. When you do, you'll never hear a word from me. I just want something to happen."

On the ride back, Dobrynin said to me, "Why don't we take that up as our special project?" Eventually we had a document that I thought was pretty good. I took that document to the president and said, "Mr. President, any lawyer would tell you that you can drive a truck through the holes in this paper, but given all the background, I believe that if we get the Pentecostals to leave the embassy, they'll be allowed to go home and eventually emigrate."

So we rolled the dice. We got the Pentecostals to leave the embassy and go home, and about two months later they were all allowed to emigrate along with their families, about sixty people in all.

The president's attitude during that meeting with Dobrynin was simple: "I just want something to happen. I won't say a word about it." My follow-up advice to him was, "The deal is that the Soviets will let them out if you don't crow." So President Reagan said nothing. How tempting it is, by contrast, for an American politician to say, "Look at what I did."

I believe these developments had an impact on President Reagan: he saw that you could make a deal with those people and they would carry it through. It probably had an impact on the Soviets, too, because they learned that they could deal with this guy and trust him. He kept his word and refrained from crowing.

This took place long before Mikhail Gorbachev appeared with his reforms. The Cold War was as cold as it could get.

Grow a Backbone

RONALD REAGAN took office with the deep sense that threatening millions of human lives and the destruction of civilization was immoral. He saw that nuclear deterrence was flawed in its very essence and that this error had led to a whole edifice of reasoning about deterrence that also was flawed.

Reagan's view was to be resolute, with no rose-colored glasses. As he said in a 1983 speech to the National Association of Evangelicals:

> So, in your discussions of the nuclear freeze proposals, I urge you to beware the temptation of pride—the temptation of blithely declaring yourselves above it all and label both sides equally at fault, to ignore the facts of history and the aggressive impulses of an evil empire, to simply call the arms race a giant misunderstanding and thereby remove yourself from the struggle between right and wrong and good and evil.

The Reagan playbook: pay attention to execution. Be realistic—if a country acts like an "evil empire," do not be afraid to say so. Be strong militarily and economically, and have a confident spirit. Develop an agenda of how you see US interests and be ready to engage on the basis of that agenda.

I brought to the table my work with the collective-bargaining system and the contracts that emerged from it. I had become increasingly impressed with the resulting system for adjudicating disputes. The system provided a fair means for adjudication. There was also a recognition that if you allowed unmanaged protests, in the form of "wildcat strikes," to succeed, you were really asking for trouble. As the saying went, "There's only one thing worse than a wildcat strike, and that's a successful wildcat strike." Then you had really lost control.

The year 1983 was the year of the missile: intense negotiations with the Soviets about intermediate-range nuclear forces (INF) and strategic forces. President Reagan set out the US agenda involving an end (zero option) to INF weapons. This proposal was considered by many to be impossible because the Soviets had 1,500 of these weapons deployed and we had none. The other negotiation track involved strategic nuclear arms, with the US proposal being a reduction to equal levels of 50 percent in their numbers. The Reagan proposals involved very large reductions, whereas previous arms talks called for limitations.

Talks seemed unproductive even though—with full consultations with our allies—we modified our positions from time to time. The talks also were marked by an abrupt departure from that concept of linkage, the détente-era strategy of connecting political and military issues. When the Soviets shot down a Korean airliner in 1983, the United States led the charge in condemning the action and demanding that it not recur. At the same time, over intense resistance within the administration, I went ahead with a scheduled meeting with Gromyko and we sent our arms negotiators back to Geneva, moving further away from linkage. These moves helped convince our European allies that our negotiating efforts were sincere.

When negotiations stalled, deployment started. Our most intense confrontation was over the deployment of the Pershing ballistic missiles in Germany. The Soviets did everything they could to fan talk of war. The Soviets then withdrew from negotiations and further stimulated talk of war. The president and our NATO allies held firm. Early in 1984, we launched a coordinated approach to easing tensions, including meetings where both US and Soviet representatives were present. I had a bilateral meeting with Gromyko that was stiff but reasonably substantive. Months wore on, tensions eased, and by August I was able to meet with the president and tell him: "At four different places in Europe, US diplomats have been approached by Soviet representatives who say virtually the same thing. We interpret the comments to mean that if Gromyko is invited to Washington as he used to be, he would accept." In other words, the Soviets blinked.

After a diplomatic minuet, Gromyko's return to the White House was arranged. I found one little vignette especially memorable—and further proof that the human element is so important.

Gromyko was scheduled to come into the West Wing, meet in the Oval Office, and then walk down the colonnade with the others. There was to be a break and then a working lunch. I asked Nancy Reagan, "How about coming to the stand-around time? You're the hostess." She agreed.

Gromyko saw Nancy Reagan and made a beeline for her. There was nobody else in the room as far as he was concerned, and they talked. All of a sudden, he said to her, "Does your husband want peace?"

Nancy bristled and said, "Of course my husband wants peace."

Gromyko said, "Well then, every night before he goes to sleep, whisper in his ear, 'peace.'"

Gromyko was taller than Nancy. She put her hands on his shoulders and pulled him down so he had to bend his knees. Then she said, "I'll whisper it in *your* ear. Peace."

The meeting turned out to be a major event and, after the 1984 election, agreement was reached for negotiations between Gromyko and me in Geneva that resulted in an agreement for the resumption of arms control talks.

On December 20, 1984, notably, Konstantin Chernenko, then ruling general secretary, sent a letter to President Reagan in which he said:

> Recently you have spoken on more than one occasion, also in your letters of November 16th and December 7th and earlier in your conversation with Andrei A. Gromyko, in favor of moving along the road leading eventually to liquidation of nuclear weapons, completely and everywhere. We, of course, welcome that. The Soviet Union, as is known, as far back as the dawn of the nuclear age came out for prohibiting and liquidating such weapons . . . it

is not yet too late to start practical movement toward this noble objective.

These developments were greeted with skepticism by the détente crowd, although our actions were certainly consistent with the peaceful coexistence idea. All this was in place before Gorbachev emerged as leader of the Soviet Union in the spring of 1984.

Support the Change You Want to See

MIKHAIL GORBACHEV emerged as leader of the Soviet Union in the spring of 1984. Our delegation met with him at the time of the funeral of his predecessor, Konstantin Chernenko. Afterward I said to our people: "This is a different kind of Soviet leader from anyone we have dealt with before. He is quicker and better informed, and he will make a more agile adversary. But you can have a conversation with him. He listens to what you say and responds and he expects you to respond to what he has to say."

The highlights of the years to come included the surprisingly productive Reagan-Gorbachev summits in Geneva—where the two leaders agreed that "a nuclear war can never be won and must never be fought"—and Reykjavik, where, among other things of profound importance, the leaders reached the first formal agreement that human rights would be a recognized subject on our agendas in Washington and Moscow. These seemed to hint at further changes to come in the Soviet system.

The big news at Reykjavik was the dramatic discussions on nuclear arms. In the end, the meeting broke up without full agreement, but I was convinced that we now had seen the Soviets' bottom line and that, sooner or later, the INF and START (Strategic Arms Reduction Treaty) agreements would be completed. That is exactly what happened. I was also convinced that President Reagan's announced efforts to develop a defense against ballistic missiles—the Strategic Defense Initiative—had a major impact on Soviet thinking.

In subsequent visits to Moscow, I could see a gradual change. The effects of glasnost and perestroika were real. Once I was invited to lunch with a group described as intellectuals. One of them had a novel that after twenty years had finally been published. Another was a producer who said he could now produce plays without censorship. I cautioned that what had been turned on could be turned off, but they all insisted, "No, the process has gone beyond the point of no return."

On that same visit, I was asked to appear on the leading talk show. I agreed, with one condition: everything I said would be broadcast. No censorship. At one point I easily worked in comments about Afghanistan: "You should get out of there. The Afghan people don't want you. You are taking casualties." To my astonishment, they kept broadcasting.

I had worked on a number of dissidents' cases, including that of a woman named Ida Nudel. I had even given her name to Eduard Shevardnadze, who said he would work on it. One afternoon my phone rang and a little voice said, "This is Ida Nudel. I'm in Jerusalem. I'm home!" I was deeply touched. Real accomplishments have a human face, in this case Ida Nudel's.

Eventually a large number of refuseniks would emigrate to Israel and the United States. I had worked on this issue going back to my first meeting with Gromyko in 1982. But as change began to emerge in the Soviet Union, I initiated, with the president's support, an argument to Shevardnadze and then Gorbachev that the future would be dominated by an information age and countries that were closed and compartmentalized would inevitably be left behind. They were interested in this argument. What part it played in the eventual change in Soviet emigration politics, I have no way of knowing, but the fact is that a big change took place.

On one occasion, the Soviet and US delegations gathered to discuss regional issues, starting with Afghanistan. Shevardnadze asked for a little time alone with me and we went into my private office. There he told me that a Soviet decision had been *made*—past tense—though not announced, to withdraw from Afghanistan. He wanted me to know this confidentially, he said, so we could work together to minimize the bloodshed that would accompany the withdrawal of Soviet troops. Here is an example of how "gardening" paid off.

Don't Give In When You're Right

PRESIDENT REAGAN'S VIEW, which I shared, was that change in the Soviet Union was extensive and real, and that the change had staying power and was worth working on and encouraging. Still skeptical were prominent students of the Soviet Union, primarily Robert Gates at the CIA. Former president Nixon, my old boss, and Henry Kissinger collaborated on an article, "To Withdraw Missiles We Must Add Conditions," published in the *Los Angeles Times* on April 26, 1987. They warned that it would be "a profound mistake" to sign the nuclear arms reduction agreement without other major Soviet concessions and cautioned against "the wrong kind of deal."

I responded that we had achieved our objective of getting rid of 1,500 Soviet missiles aimed at our European and Asian allies. In a long and careful article published in *Time,* I argued that "NATO would retain a robust deterrent" of modern weapons, integrated command, and preparedness, including three hundred thousand US troops poised in Europe. The deal, I wrote, would "continue to deter Soviet adventurism on the continent."

Despite the fact that the Intermediate-Range Nuclear Forces (INF) treaty offered a result at first thought impossible to achieve, along with an unprecedented level of on-site inspections and firsthand congressional monitoring of the negotiations, we took nothing for granted as far as ratification by the Senate was concerned.

Beyond formal testimony before the Foreign Relations and Armed Services committees, some of us met informally with large and small groups of senators. President Reagan, of course, gave the treaty strong and total support. In the end, the effort paid off. The final vote for ratification was 93–5.

Many of the lessons of this negotiating process touch on statecraft but go beyond it:

- Leadership from the top (in this case, the president) is irreplaceable.
- Negotiate from a position of clear (US) interest.
- Listen to opposing views but don't compromise or accommodate views you deem incorrect, even when those views are expressed by justifiably esteemed critics.
- Realize that any negotiation is part of an evolving general environment on which you must work continuously.
- Pay attention to those you need on your side (e.g., members of Congress) as you go along, remembering the maxim "If you want me in on the landing, include me in the takeoff."

Years later at Stanford, after we had both left office, I asked Mikhail Gorbachev, "What was the turning point in the end of the Cold War?"

"Reykjavik," he said, "because the two leaders talked for two full days about all the important issues." Then he asked for my opinion.

"The deployment of INF missiles," I replied, "especially in Germany." We and our NATO allies showed we could take strong action on a genuinely cohesive basis. This was a true show of strength, in many ways more important than the use of force.

But I had also listened carefully to Gorbachev's speech at the United Nations on December 7, 1988. There he had publicly announced the hard news: the intention to draw back conventional forces in Europe. For my money, the real news was the clear tone in which he announced, without really saying so, that the Cold War was over.

Beyond pulling back a half-million soldiers and thousands of tanks, Gorbachev in that speech also explicitly endorsed the "common interest of mankind" (no longer the class struggle) as the basis of Soviet foreign policy. Most significant for Eastern Europe, he declared "the compelling necessity of the principle of freedom of choice" as "a universal principle to which there should be no exceptions."

Senator Daniel Patrick Moynihan called his speech "the most astounding statement of surrender in the history of ideological struggle." Retired general Andrew Goodpaster, a former NATO commander and top aide to President Eisenhower, described Gorbachev's announcement of unilateral troop cuts as "the most significant step since NATO was founded."

I felt sure, reporting to the president after hearing the speech, that the Cold War was over. All that was left was to manage the end game with a dose of common sense.

After the UN speech, Gorbachev came for a farewell luncheon with President Reagan and me. By this time, attention had shifted to the former vice president, now president-elect, George H. W. Bush. As our discussion was coming to an end, President Reagan took me aside and said, "What's wrong with George?"

Apparently the new president was uneasy because he had decided on a pause in developments with the Soviets. His national security team, in particular Brent Scowcroft and Robert Gates, had convinced him, as he remarked, that he "would like to build on what President Reagan had done" but "would need a little time to review the issues." Bush described the theory behind his new team as "to revitalize things by putting in new people."

But the new Bush advisers were more than skeptical of Gorbachev. In subsequent memoirs, national security adviser Scowcroft dismissed the UN speech when he described his staunch opposition to any early summit with Gorbachev in 1989:

Unless there were substantive accomplishments, such as arms control, the Soviets would be able to capitalize on the one outcome left—the good feelings generated by the meeting. They would use the resulting euphoria to undermine Western resolve, and a sense of complacency would encourage some to believe the United States could relax its vigilance. The Soviets in general and Gorbachev in particular were masters at creating these enervating atmospheres. Gorbachev's UN speech had established, with a largely rhetorical flourish, a heady atmosphere of optimism. He could exploit an early meeting with a new president as evidence to declare the Cold War over without providing substantive actions from a "new" Soviet Union. Under the circumstances which prevailed [in 1989], I believed an early summit would only abet the current Soviet propaganda campaign.

Later I learned that Gorbachev had envisioned his speech as an "anti-Fulton"—a bookend of sorts to Winston Churchill's historic "Iron Curtain" speech of 1946 in Fulton, Missouri, at the dawn of the Cold War. The proffered troop and weapons reductions, in Gorbachev's mind, would build trust and open the way for quick progress with the new American administration led by President Bush. Anatoly Chernyaev, Gorbachev's foreign policy adviser, wrote: "Much has been written about the impression that Gorbachev made on the world in his UN speech. But we also have to consider the impact on him of the world's response to his speech. . . . Having received such broad recognition and support, having been 'certified' a world-class leader of great authority, he could be faster and surer in shaking off the fetters of the past in all aspects of foreign policy."

Regrettably, exactly those "fetters of the past" continued to restrain the highest levels of the new Bush administration from meeting Gorbachev halfway. Arguably, they postponed dramatic reductions in nuclear weapons, fissile materials, and conventional armaments, to the detriment of international security today.

As time passed, momentum reasserted itself, particularly as the new secretary of state, James Baker, forged a strong working relationship, as I had, with the Soviet foreign minister, Shevardnadze. In the end, the Bush team managed the end game of the Cold War with great skill, avoiding the temptation to cry victory and thereby stiffen opposition to further progress.

Be a Team Player

TWO DAYS before I left office, I was honored at a lunch organized by Ted Kennedy (D-Mass) and Dick Lugar (R-Ind) and presided over by Senate leaders Bob Dole and George Mitchell. The senators expressed thanks for being consulted so many times and I expressed my gratitude for all their ideas and support. I was deeply moved by the award they gave me, as I was the following day when President Reagan, in his final official event in the White House, gave Mike Mansfield and me the Presidential Medal of Freedom. The president said I had "helped to make the world a freer and more peaceful place."

He said:

George Shultz has been a Marine, an academic, a businessman, and a public servant. He has held four cabinet-level posts, distinguishing himself as a secretary of labor, director of the Office of Management and Budget, treasury secretary, and finally as one of America's great secretaries of state. Over the last six and a half years, in managing our foreign policy, he has served wisely and met great challenges and great opportunities.

My response:

Mr. President . . . there's a phrase that's catching on: "the Reagan years." There's a ring to it. And, Mr. President, it is the ring of freedom. You have advocated it, fought for it. You have known that the price of freedom is eternal vigilance. You have known this is a matter of principle on which you don't compromise. You have known that there are times when it requires action—sometimes, at least initially, not necessarily popular action—but you have to do it.

You have also known—and I've heard you say many times—that the strength comes from "We the People," that we get our legitimacy and you get your legitimacy as president from the people. And you've never been in any doubt, and none of us have, about who we came here to serve: the American people.

After the ceremony, I was surprised when I returned to my office and found another reception. Paul Nitze described the scene in his memoir *From Hiroshima to Glasnost: At the Center of Decision*:

When the secretary and Mrs. Shultz returned from a farewell luncheon at which the President awarded him the Medal of Freedom, we were awaiting him in his office. Mike presented him with the Jefferson medal, read the citation, and then read a number of witty, moving letters from the secretary's friends, including Prime Minister Thatcher, Chairman Gorbachev, Chancellor Kohl, and others. Thereafter several of us in the State Department had an opportunity to speak. Having been in the government longer than others, I was accorded the privilege of speaking first. My remarks were as follows:

"Mr. Secretary, for us old-timers in the government, these years serving in your State Department have been unique. Within a week after you took over, it was evident that the Shultz regime would be different. The aim would be team play, not bureaucratic infighting. What would count was initiative, energy, and courage. We were confident that you would back us up if we ran into personal opposition for pursuing forward-leaning ideas.

"Over the years your thoughts, ideas, and integrity prevailed, thus steadily enhancing the opportunity for constructive work by you and all members of your team.

"The results are there for everyone to see. They cover every aspect of world affairs. The centerpiece has been Western relationships with the Soviet Union and its associates. Six years ago the relationships were wholly adversarial and restricted to trying to make the military aspects of that relationship less immediately dangerous. Gradually you managed to expand the scope and depth of the dialogue. By persistence you raised human rights from a taboo subject to the forefront of the dialogue. You brought regional issues into the realm of productive discussion. Some of the bilateral issues were solved; others have become more manageable. On the arms control front, from concrete achievement on INF you have opened wide the scope of achievable success across the board from START, defense, and space, to balance in conventional forces in Europe and the outlawing of chemical and biological weapons.

"What are the elements of character and leadership that have made that possible? I would list them as follows: being wholly comfortable within your own skin, a commonsense approach to problems, forthrightness in your relations with others, confidence in the United States and the fundamental ideas informing its spirit.

"The result has been that those of us who have been fortunate to be part of your team have been part of a great experience. We deeply thank you for it."

I was deeply moved by Paul's comments and those of President Reagan and others over the previous two days. But I also reflected on what I had learned from Bemis. It's not just what you know, but what you realize, largely thanks to experience.

PART SIX

Transitions

Bring It All Together

IT WAS EASY and pleasant to transition from secretary of state to member of the Stanford faculty. It became a time to reflect, for our family to enjoy sunny California, and to revel in a truly stimulating environment.

I became a professor (soon to be emeritus professor) at the Graduate School of Business. I also became the Thomas W. and Susan B. Ford Distinguished Fellow at the Hoover Institution, which provides me with great facilities for research and writing. I wrote *Turmoil and Triumph: My Years as Secretary of State*, a major effort. Another book, *Issues and Action*, accompanied a three-part PBS documentary on my life. I co-authored, with John Shoven, the book *Putting Our House in Order: A Guide to Social Security and Health Care Reform*. A subsequent book, *Issues on My Mind*, included narrative and reprints of some of my past speeches and writings. *Game Changers: Energy on the Move*, a book produced with Robert Armstrong of MIT, reflects my interests in research and development in the energy field.

Amid all this activity, other issues also came to the fore in my thinking and attitudes.

I could now draw on a considerable variety of deep experiences from my Marine Corps years on through exciting times at MIT, the University of Chicago, the Bechtel Corporation, and leadership of four cabinet-level posts, all expanding the scope of what I realized as well as what I knew.

Several now-familiar themes always emerge:

- Early in my life and at a very simple level, I came to realize how competition in the marketplace brings on creativity. And, of course, that very creativity is at the heart of much of American success.

- I realized from my Marine Corps experience how important it is to do what you say you're going to do. As my sergeant told me, never point a rifle at anybody unless you're willing to pull the trigger. Empty threats deprive anything you say of real meaning. The other side of that coin is that as you negotiate deals or work with people on issues, always do what you say you're going to do. Then people trust you, and trust is the coin of the realm.

- Organizations work best when there is accountability combined with an opportunity to be a participant. A participant is a part-owner and the eye of the owner, even a part-time owner, is a constructive and accountable eye.

- Government service is a great opportunity to make a difference and therefore a great privilege, but you cannot want the job too much. You have to be true to yourself, and if you find yourself where an important policy within your purview goes against your views of what is right, you should resign.

- Government intervention such as bailouts of companies in trouble have long-term and undesirable consequences, so they should be minimized so that expectations do not change behavior.

- There is a playbook for negotiating about things big and small. You have to make sure you can accomplish what you set out to accomplish—execution matters; be realistic (throw away those rose-colored glasses); be strong, not just militarily and economically but with will and purpose, too; develop your agenda (don't think about the other guy's agenda, or you will end up negotiating with yourself); and, finally, be ready to engage on the basis of your agenda.

- Diversity is everywhere and growing. This is an age when people know what's going on and can organize, so you must confront the problem of governing over diversity in an age of transparency.

- Many of the most important problems can be resolved only on an international basis. Thus it is essential to be able to reach out to others. Examples of these challenges are as big as they come: the proliferation and danger of use of nuclear weapons, the potential consequences of a warming climate, and the threat to the state system of governance posed by important players, the Islamic State of Iraq and al-Sham (ISIS) in particular, who defy that system but have wide appeal.

- As you work on individual issues, always be aware that the general environment makes a big difference as you hunt for solutions. The twilight of the Cold War meant arms control deals were possible, large numbers of Soviet Jews were able to emigrate, Cuban troops would leave Angola (a key step in ending apartheid in South Africa), and so on. So when we work on individual issues, we have to try to anticipate the impact of a world awash in change.

- Leadership always matters. It is a key to success—perhaps not the only key but always a huge part of accomplishing difficult things. I have observed terrific leadership in universities, companies, and government. A good father is a good leader, too. We should do everything possible to develop these capacities.

- Organizations stay healthy by realizing that departing leaders have a final responsibility: helping to prepare their successors, in every conceivable way, for their own success. No leader lasts forever. I have seen enough really good transitions to realize fully how important they are. I have also seen a few occasions when the outgoing official thought his performance would look better if the incoming official stumbled. That is irresponsible, but it happens all too often.

Progress Can Slip Away

BY GOOD FORTUNE I met Sid Drell, a leading physicist, when I arrived at Stanford, and we became close friends. We both worried about the potential impact of nuclear weapons and, of course, I carried forward the Reagan idea of finding our way to a world without nuclear weapons.

"A nuclear war can never be won and must never be fought," President Reagan had said in his 1984 State of the Union address. Again I recall that surprisingly constructive meeting between him and Mikhail Gorbachev in Geneva in 1985 when they jointly echoed that statement.

Reagan and Gorbachev agreed on the goal of a world free of nuclear weapons. Implementing that goal was something else again, but we did achieve the elimination of intermediate-range nuclear weapons and the reduction by half of nuclear weapons with strategic range. So, by the end of the twentieth century, the number of nuclear weapons in the world was one-third as high as at the time of the 1986 Reykjavik meeting between Reagan and Gorbachev.

We seemed to be in a golden moment by the time the Cold War ended—a security and economic commons characterized the world environment. In 2006, Sid Drell and I organized a conference at the Hoover Institution to commemorate the twentieth anniversary of the Reykjavik meeting. Out of that event came an article that I wrote with former secretary of state Henry Kissinger, former secretary of defense William Perry, and former chairman of the Senate Armed Services Committee Sam Nunn. Published in the *Wall Street Journal*, the article called for a world free of nuclear weapons and identified steps needed to get there. We urged "a bold initiative consistent with America's moral heritage. . . . Without the bold vision, the actions will not be perceived as fair or urgent. Without the actions, the vision will not be perceived as realistic or possible."

Response was swift and enthusiastic. In the presidential campaign leading up to the 2008 election, we were pleased that both candidates, Senators Barack Obama and John McCain, endorsed our view, so we felt the objective was nonpartisan. Since that time, President Obama has advocated that view and has convened four conferences at the head-of-state level designed to achieve the vital objective of getting control of fissile material.

But the atmosphere on a global basis has soured. Our group continues to point out the dangers of reliance on deterrence, but to our alarm, progress has stopped and movement toward proliferation of the most destructive weapons is again a problem.

As our group wrote in the *Wall Street Journal* on March 7, 2011:

As long as there has been war, there have been efforts to deter actions a nation considers threatening. Until fairly recently, this meant building a military establishment capable of intimidating the adversary, defeating him or making his victory more costly than the projected gains. This, with conventional weapons, took time. Deterrence and war strategy were identical.

But the advent of the nuclear weapon introduced entirely new factors. It was possible, for the first time, to inflict at the beginning of a war the maximum casualties.

Potential warfare aside, we also stress the fact that since 1950 thirty-two incidents have been reported worldwide in which the safety of nuclear weapons was compromised. By now people should realize how foolish it is to link the safety and well-being of humanity to the idea that nuclear weapons can be used as deterrents with a total lack of mistakes or errors in judgment.

Out of office and out of Washington, I and my good friends and colleagues Sid Drell, Henry Kissinger, Bill Perry, and Sam Nunn try to keep the flame burning so that when and if the global atmosphere improves, the ideas stand ready to help lessen our dependence on nuclear weapons with their ability to wipe out humanity.

From the beginning of our appeals, my colleagues and I have stressed that the world is complicated. We highlight the regional conflicts that would have to be settled. We point out that a world without nuclear weapons would not be the world as it is, minus nuclear weapons. Steps to create the *conditions* for a world without nuclear weapons cannot be ignored. For instance, conflicts have driven decisions to acquire nuclear weapons in Northeast Asia, South Asia, and the Middle East.

One of President Obama's prime goals after he took office was a new US-Russian treaty to reduce the numbers of nuclear warheads. His team succeeded in negotiating a treaty dubbed New START, which the Senate ratified in 2010 by a 71–26 vote. It created a new and very effective verification system and mandated a modest reduction in strategic nuclear weapons.

But the atmosphere is different. So now I ask two questions: What can we learn from observing the forces that led to the golden moment when huge reductions in nuclear arsenals took place? Can we identify the key requirements of a road toward a world free of nuclear weapons?

Here are some insights from that golden moment.

We began with a deep, long-held sense of unease about the devastating power of nuclear weapons. The 1986 Chernobyl nuclear power-plant accident, though it involved a reactor and not a weapon, reinforced this feeling. I was impressed that in my first meeting with Gorbachev after Chernobyl, I found that he had asked the same question I put to my colleagues in the United States: what is the relationship between the vast damage we see at Chernobyl and what would have been produced by a weapon? The answer: a weapon would be even more devastating, by far. Today, the aftermath of the 2011 tsunami-caused disaster at the Fukushima nuclear plant in Japan continues to breed similar anxiety, but somehow it seems easier for the world to ignore the nuclear risk and sleep at night. So the sense of danger, unfortunately all too real, needs to be kept in public view.

Moreover, leverage is needed. It might seem paradoxical, but President Reagan's Strategic Defense Initiative provided such leverage in the final years of the Soviet Union. Consider this statement from a lengthy letter written by Reagan to Gorbachev on July 25, 1986, after the Geneva meeting but before the Reykjavik meeting:

> Significant commitments of this type with respect to strategic defense would make sense only if made in conjunction with the implementation of *immediate actions on both sides to begin moving toward our common goal of the total elimination of nuclear weapons* [emphasis added]. Toward this goal, I believe we also share the view that the process must begin with radical and stabilizing reductions in the offensive nuclear arsenals of both the United States and the Soviet Union.

We also need people at the helm of key countries who can think big, act boldly, *and* carry their constituencies with them. This is difficult and takes a leader who will stand up to fierce opposition from a respected source.

I vividly remember coming back to Washington from Reykjavik and practically being summoned to the British ambassador's residence. There, my friend Margaret Thatcher "handbagged" me.

"George," she said, "how could you sit there and allow the president to talk about a world free of nuclear weapons?"

I said, "But Margaret, he's the president."

"Yes, but you're supposed to be the one with his feet on the ground."

"But Margaret, I agreed with him."

The idea was probably too bold for immediate implementation, but it was out there. Some down payments emerged. The Senate voted 93–5, for instance, to ratify the INF Treaty eliminating intermediate-range nuclear weapons.

The final requirement, the real key, is a change in atmosphere. With Reykjavik and the steps that followed, the Cold War came to an end, so whatever existing justifications there were for nuclear weapons diminished. People even began to look at the financial burden and think about how the money spent on nuclear weapons could be better used.

So, what does this tell us about the road ahead? How can we protect the progress won in those days?

First, we must have the ideas in place that can help us reach our goal, step by step. The ideas are there; they need to be publicized. For example, we have made great strides in the ability to verify numbers and deployment of weapons. Experts are working to get better control of fissile material. Negotiators are reaching agreements on verification, such as in the breathtaking arrangements for on-site inspection in the most recent US-Russia START treaty. And progress is appearing along parallel tracks such as the Treaty on Open Skies, a mechanism of unarmed surveillance flights, developed by Sid Drell and Chris Stubbs.

Second, hard work obviously must take place on nuclear proliferation by Iran (enforce the deal) and North Korea, and on sources of great tension such as the confrontation between Pakistan and India.

Third, we need to acknowledge that the great post–World War II activation of a global security and economic commons is deteriorating badly, and that we now find ourselves in a world awash in change. This deterioration generates uncertainty—and uncertainty causes people to cling to whatever they think, rightly or wrongly, will give them security.

Diversity, long in existence but suppressed, is asserting itself as a problem of governance as never before. It is surging in a world of transparency—a world dominated by the information and communications revolution. A return to a stable global economic and security commons means learning how to govern over diversity in this age of transparency. I will focus on this problem in the pages ahead.

Finally, and of immense importance, is continued advocacy. Religious leaders are gathering behind the broad conviction that weapons of mass destruction are inhumane and incompatible with the basic principles of any religion. Bishop William Swing's United Religions Initiative (URI) now has a presence in ninety-five countries. People of different religions come together in "cooperation circles" to discuss common problems, including the dangers posed by nuclear weapons.

There are other voices, too. The Nuclear Threat Initiative (NTI) has produced a compelling documentary on nuclear weapons, and an effort is under way to organize influential groups in every part of the world. The Comprehensive Test Ban Treaty still awaits ratification by the Senate. We all need to keep ourselves informed and make ourselves heard in a sustained, focused way.

Time is not on our side. I hope and pray we do not have to wait until a modern nuclear weapon is used before we teach ourselves, perhaps too late, that these weapons can never be accepted.

Never Lose Sight of the Bottom Line

I CONTINUE with my enduring interest in economics and economic policy, especially into how tax, spending, and regulatory arrangements hold back the economy. This theme resonates back to my days as chairman of Ronald Reagan's Economic Policy Advisory Board during the presidential primaries, the campaign, and his first year in office. I also have long-standing concerns about health care and education, again with an economics foundation.

At Hoover I have had the privilege of working closely with outstanding colleagues, most notably John Taylor, John Cogan, Michael Boskin, John Shoven, John Cochrane, Eric Hanushek, and Scott Atlas. We put our heads together and try to find ways to make a difference in US policymaking.

I worry deeply about the inadequacy of the K–12 education system for too many of our young people, and I have become convinced of the importance of school choice. If parents and children can go to the school of their choice, schools will be forced to compete for students, with beneficial results. My time with the late and inspirational Milton Friedman convinces me that school choice is the best way forward.

Health care, too, is of central importance to all Americans. Everyone must have access to the system, and that access is an important achievement of the Affordable Care Act. Reservations about this law grow out of its complexity and its top-down, mandated approach. Anyone with experience in wage and price controls recognizes another stubborn problem: the effort to control costs that way has a tendency to reduce the supply of health care providers. Many health care providers are dropping out of the system, so we reduce supply while increasing demand.

To maintain the promise of the Affordable Care Act—that everyone is covered—Medicare and Medicaid could be authorized to provide adequate health savings accounts to their clients. Such savings accounts put resources in the hands of patients. They are part of the increased movement toward prevention, a trend I applaud, accompanied by efforts to make people more directly responsible for their own health. Again, though, for this responsibility to be exercised effectively, patients need direct access to information about preventive measures and about prices and outcomes.

I have had time to ponder how to bring many of these points together. For instance, in a 2014 *Wall Street Journal* article headlined "How to Get America Moving Again," I wrote:

> Admiral Isoroku Yamamoto, who led the Japanese fleet at Pearl Harbor, had spent some time before World War II in the United States. After the attack, he allegedly said, with a sense of foreboding, "I fear all we have done is to awaken a sleeping giant and fill him with a terrible resolve." Well, the giant is sleeping again. What does it take to wake us up? How many times can we be kicked in the belly before we take notice?
>
> The world is awash in change that affects us and our allies. We must recognize this and strengthen our military capabilities, set effective strategies, and be prepared to support our principles and oppose those who seek to destroy them. To do so, we must get our economy really rolling again. How? Everyone knows how. We just need to take action:
>
> 1. Cleanse the personal income tax system of deductions and lower the marginal rate on a revenue-neutral basis. The template is right there in the 1986 Tax Act, which passed the US Senate 97–3.
> 2. We all know that corporate taxation is an anachronism. Why do we want a system that encourages American companies to reincorporate abroad? Let the earnings they make in other countries be taxed there, and that's it. . . . And let's

      lower the corporate tax rate to be competitive with the rest of the world. How about 20 percent?

3. We all know that the maze and uncertainty of the regulatory octopus is stifling the economy. Regulations . . . can be made simpler and designed to work better. Overhaul the current complexity so that even small businesses can see how to comply without having to hire compliance advocates they can't afford.

4. While we are reducing uncertainty, why not take the mystery out of the Federal Reserve? The Fed can establish a rules-based monetary policy with the ability to deviate from the rules as long as it publicly explains why, using cost-benefit thinking.

5. Get control of spending. Otherwise the burden of servicing government debt when normal interest rates return—a burden that already amounts to hundreds of billions annually—will be unbearable. . . .

There are many well-known ways to put the Social Security system back on track so it will be there for young people in the future. One way is to change from wage-indexing to price-indexing as a method of calculating benefits, and apply the change only to people under the age of fifty-five. That means younger people will receive benefits at least as large as those now being paid with protection against any future inflation. Another change is to index the normal retirement age—when people can receive full benefits—to longevity. And when workers reach that age, stop any payroll deductions and employer contributions to encourage them to stay in the labor force. Their pay will increase and they will be less costly employees. Incentives work. . . .

6. Insurance is about risk. The main risks in the health care area are catastrophic events that have high costs, so high-

deductible catastrophic insurance is what is needed. Even young people will buy such coverage. . . . Most people who make a decent living can afford to put pretax income into health savings accounts, which they can then use to pay for routine medical services. We also should tweak Medicare and Medicaid so that significant health savings accounts can be created for their recipients. . . . Consumers need more information about the prices of health care services so they can make informed decisions. Finally, we should encourage public and private neighborhood health clinics, which are spreading rapidly and can dispense health care inexpensively. . . .

What about our defense and foreign policy? Let's put our military to work figuring out what we really need. We want no-nonsense people in charge. We want to do away with all nonsensical across-the-board sequester rules. But we must have a robust military capability. And then we need to conduct ourselves in a credible way. . . .

The threats to us and our friends are real. So, wake up, sleeping giant! You have work to do.

A second *Journal* article, co-written in 2012 with Hoover colleague Eric Hanushek, touched on education and a prominent issue of the day, income inequality:

Too often we neglect a key ingredient of our nation's economic future: the human capital produced by our K–12 school system. An improved education system would lead to a dramatically different future for the United States because educational outcomes strongly affect economic growth and the distribution of income. . . .

We have long benefited from our commitment to the free movement of labor and capital, strong property rights, a limited degree of government intrusion in the economy, and strong colleges and universities. But each of these advantages has eroded considerably. . . . Current US students—the future labor force—are no longer competitive with students across the developed world.

In the OECD's Programme for International Student Assessment (PISA) rankings for 2009, the United States was thirty-first in math—indistinguishable from Portugal or Italy. In "advanced" performance on math, sixteen countries produced twice as many high achievers per capita as the United States did. If we accept this level of performance, we will surely find ourselves on a low-growth path.

This doesn't have to be our fate. Imagine a school improvement program that made us competitive with Canada in math performance (which means scoring approximately 40 points higher on PISA tests) over the next twenty years. As these Canadian-skill-level students entered the labor force, they would produce a faster-growing economy.

How much faster? The results are stunning. The improvement in GDP over the next eighty years would exceed a present value of $70 trillion. That's equivalent to an average 20 percent boost in income for every US worker each year over his or her entire career. This would generate enough revenue to easily solve the US debt problem that is the object of so much current debate. . . .

Greater educational disparity leads to greater income-distribution disparity. If we fail to reform our K–12 education system, we'll be locking in inequality problems that will plague us for decades if not generations to come.

Anyone worried about income disparity in America should be deeply disturbed. The failure of the K–12 education system for so many students means that issues associated with income distribution—including higher taxes and less freedom in labor and capital markets—will be an ever-present and distressing aspect of our future. . . .

By not insisting on immediate and widespread reform we are forgoing substantial growth in our standard of living. The problem is obvious. The stakes are enormous. The solutions are within our reach.

Prepare for the Worst, Aim for the Best

EARLIER I told a story about trying to tackle the oil-import ceiling, creating a splendid strategic analysis, and being brought up short by a lack of urgency. Energy has long presented problems to American leaders and policymakers. I worked on many energy problems while in office, including, with President Reagan, the Montreal Protocol, which dealt successfully with the problem of depletion of the ozone layer. Not all energy problems are created equal, though. I must express my concern up front about the changing world climate and its potential dramatic consequences. With the climate-change problem, unlike many others, a lack of urgency could mean catastrophe.

President Nixon signed legislation creating the Environmental Protection Agency in 1970. At the time, I was head of the Office of Management and Budget, which had the task of helping the new agency get started. I found that several of the bright young people who were working for me on the oil-import task force were very eager to get jobs in the new EPA. I listened to them talk about all the environmental problems they thought could be easily identified and corrected. Their enthusiasm was infectious.

The 1973 Arab oil boycott, which our task force had more or less predicted, was traumatic for the United States. It also made it possible, as I mentioned, for good ideas about energy to be put into practice. In time it became very clear how important it would be to have someone in government—a leader, an agency—who took the environmental issue seriously and kept at it all the time.

When I was secretary of state, we heard from a lot of scientists that the ozone layer was being depleted, which raised concerns about increased human exposure to harmful radiation. There were also some perfectly respectable people who doubted any depletion was taking place. As it is today, there were people who thought there was a broad environmental problem and there were doubters. They all agreed, however, that the worst outcome could be disastrous.

I talked the problem over carefully with President Reagan during our twice-weekly private meetings. The president thought of a way to move forward. Rather than say to those with whom we disagreed, "You're villains, you're wrong," and get bogged down in finger-pointing, he would put his arm around them and say, "OK, we respect you. You have a different opinion. But we both agree this environmental problem could lead to catastrophe. How about getting together and writing an insurance policy?"

It turns out that quite often in the United States, when it's clear that some serious effort is about to start, the scientific and entrepreneurial juices start flowing and something happens. In this case, DuPont found a way to take concrete action, not just talk. The company moved swiftly to phase out the chemicals implicated in damage to the ozone layer. Then we convened a big meeting that resulted in the Montreal Protocol, signed in 1987, to protect the atmosphere. President Reagan called the result a "magnificent achievement." Twenty-five years later, the protocol has been ratified by all UN states.

I mention this episode because the current reflex in political discourse is to villainize those who oppose you. You don't try to look for common ground or how adversaries can get something accomplished. You run the other way. The scientists who worried about the ozone layer were right, and the Montreal Protocol was forged just in time. The insurance policy saved the day.

At the Hoover Institution, we have been working with Admiral Gary Roughead, recently retired as chief of naval operations. He has started a task force on the Arctic, where a new ocean is being created, something that hasn't happened since the end of the last ice age. What will be the consequences for navigation, for the environment, for resources, for national security, and for international law?

Being part of the task force impresses on me that the climate is changing and severe consequences await. Maybe you like the science;

maybe you don't. But use your eyes: Greenland is losing billions of tons of ice every year; large parts of the West Antarctic ice sheet are sliding into a warming ocean; widespread melting is beginning to threaten the water supplies of great stretches of the Earth's population.

"OK," you might say, "I agree with you that the climate is changing, but we don't know why." I would go back to the Montreal Protocol. "Why don't we take out an insurance policy? Because if it really does warm a lot, you can anticipate a huge number of consequences. Some are tolerable but some are really dire, so we should be doing something."

An insurance policy, a reasonable one, would not be that expensive. It consists basically of two simple things. The first is significant, sustained support for energy research and development, such as that going on at MIT and Stanford, where I am involved. When MIT's Bob Armstrong and I edited a book titled *Game Changers*, we wrote to many other universities where researchers are at work and collected some of their most promising results. Our book identified game-changing advances. Energy R&D deserves sustained support; currently the amount of federal dollars dedicated to it is trivial relative to government spending levels. Private money is flowing in at two to three times the government level.

The second piece of the insurance policy is a revenue-neutral carbon tax. I say to market-oriented conservatives, "Look, this is better than the government telling you to do this, this, and this. Why don't you set a substantial price and let the market react to the price? And if you make it revenue neutral, it's not taking any money out of the economy. There's no fiscal drag and you're really leveling the playing field." That's the other side of my program.

British Columbia has had a revenue-neutral carbon tax for five years that seems to be working reasonably well. It's interesting that the real per capita growth of the province's economy is slightly better than that of Canada as a whole. On that evidence, you can't argue that a revenue-neutral carbon tax is ruinous to the economy. Of course, British Columbia is small and has a lot of hydropower, but it's one example.

Recently retired senator Jeff Bingaman, former chairman of the Senate Energy Committee, and I held a colloquium at Stanford about what the states are doing on energy issues. We expanded the material into a little book called the *State Clean Energy Cookbook*. States (both red and blue) are doing a lot to advance clean, responsible energy. They are concrete examples of Justice Brandeis's laboratories of democracy.

Strength and Diplomacy Harmonize

REFLECTING ON MY TIME as secretary of state, I worry about the state of the world and how to improve the quality of intergovernmental relations and the process of governance. I am blessed at the Hoover Institution with many friends who offer deep knowledge and experience in national security issues: Sid Drell, Condoleezza Rice, Bill Perry, Jim Mattis, Gary Roughead, Jim Ellis, Jim Goodby, David Holloway, Abe Sofaer. Where to start on this most vital issue?

The first step always is to show that we can achieve what we set out to achieve. The capacity to execute must always be on display. The following example had an impact around the world.

Early in Ronald Reagan's presidency, the US air controllers went on strike. People who came into the Oval Office counseled the president that this presented very complex problems. He said: "It's not complicated at all. It's simple. They took an oath of office and they broke it. They're out." People all over the world thought Reagan was crazy, but he turned to his secretary of transportation, Drew Lewis, who had been the chief executive of a large transportation company and who understood the problems and knew how to execute, to keep the planes flying. All over the world, people thought, "This guy plays for keeps. Be careful."

The other enduring lessons embrace realism, strength and confidence, knowing what you want to achieve, alertness to opportunities, and avoiding empty threats.

Clearly, strength and diplomacy are not alternatives but rather are complementary. Diplomacy without strength is a loser; strength without diplomacy can erode because it lacks meaning.

Diversity Demands Transparency

GOVERNANCE is changing rapidly. We see an explosion in the availability of information and the ability of people to communicate, even across international boundaries. With only minimal effort, people anywhere can find out almost anything. There is no going back to a world of limited information or communication, a world where diverse interests could be ignored.

Diversity expresses itself in many ways: in religion, ethnicity, color, economic well-being, and the ability to express oneself. Changes in the way the world is governed can be liberating for the people being governed, especially if their interests have not been recognized before. Autocratic and corrupt governments are more easily exposed. In Ukraine, for example, a deal with Russia by the pro-Russian government was quickly exposed as contrary to the interests of the citizens and the prospect for greater prosperity and the rule of law. In 2014 the upheaval displaced Prime Minister Viktor Yanukovich.

On the whole, new information and communication technologies enhance the freedom for individuals to think for themselves, to believe whatever they want to believe, and to question whatever is taking place. A new freedom emerges to question and even replace ruling authorities.

At the same time, from the standpoint of anyone charged with the responsibility of governance, the fragmentation and the power of dissident groups can easily swamp the coherence needed for effective governance. The ability to challenge authority, even legitimate authority, can easily extend to actions that may be good for the populace as a whole but less beneficial for a part of it. That part now demands to be heard.

Those who are governing need to be able to recognize the diversity among those they oversee and learn how to work with it, allowing diversity to express itself as long as that expression is not disruptive to the whole. Not least of the issues of diversity is refugee movement: Europe, for instance, has more refugees than at any time since the end of World War II. This broad movement will challenge ideas of assimilation and the structures of age-old peoples and civilizations.

Even in an information age, not all information is correct. We must come up with checks and balances to ensure that facts square with reality. The declining importance of traditional news media, which try hard to check facts and be sure what they publish is correct, can work against dissemination of good information.

Moreover, the new tools of information are also placed in the hands of those who would do society harm. Criminal networks and terrorists can more easily organize themselves and spread their doctrines. Many of the new problems that arise will yield only to international efforts.

At Home in the United States of Diversity

IMAGINE CHRISTMAS NIGHT, 1776. General Washington stands in his boat crossing the Delaware with his statesman's vision and his saber, a soldier's strength. Lieutenant James Monroe holds a flag against the winter storm. Others in the small boat are an apparently mismatched group of people from all over the struggling new country, not yet the United States of America:

> In the bow, a rifleman from the West in deerskin leggings
> Behind him, a black sailor from New England
> A recent Scottish immigrant wearing a cap from the Scots-English wars
> A Baltimore merchant wearing the insignia of a volunteer Maryland regiment
> A frontiersman, perhaps from Kentucky
> A woman, pulling an oar
> A soldier, in full uniform, from a Delaware regiment
> A Pennsylvania farmer with a countryman's double-barreled shotgun
> A Southerner who is clearly ill
> In the stern, wearing a beaded pouch, an Indian
> Finally, out of sight, with only his bayonet showing, an unknown person. (If you, the viewer of this painting, do not see one of your people in the boat, you can imagine yourself as this unidentified person.)
> In all, with General Washington and Lieutenant Monroe, thirteen people in the boat represent the thirteen colonies.

This inspiring painting, which hangs in the Metropolitan Museum of Art in New York, sets forth the basic problem of governance. People from thirteen colonies exhibit their differences, and one of

General Washington's great contributions to our Revolution was his ability to pull people with different experiences and viewpoints into the joint pursuit of a common vision. Washington was governing over diversity in the face of a well-equipped adversary and a Continental Congress that failed to meet his army's needs. His capacity for governance was severely tested. Fortunately for our fledgling country, his leadership was magnificent.

As the father of our country, George Washington went on to participate in writing the Constitution and take part in forming our new government. He and his fellow participants in the Constitutional Convention realized that success would depend on recognizing that they had thirteen very different states on their hands. They designed a form of government that was unique in its time.

A federal government was established, but with limited power. That power was checked and balanced by the creation of executive, judicial, and legislative branches, as the framers wanted to avoid the possibility of concentrated authority. The legislature itself consisted of two distinct bodies: the House, with representatives reflecting populations and acting by majority rule, and the Senate, which gave each state two votes, so that small states could not be dominated by large. At the very birth of our country those wise citizens understood the problem of governing over diversity. The Constitution also required that certain processes, such as ratification of treaties, receive a two-thirds vote in the Senate.

As the federal government had limited power that was checked and balanced, the basic functions of governance affecting daily life were allocated to state and local governments and to individuals themselves. All of this was in recognition of the need to govern over the diversity of the new United States, acknowledging differences and providing an overlay of common purpose and the potential for integrated activity.

Religion too would be seen as pluralistic. The United States came into being as a nation of the Enlightenment, designed in the Federalist Papers and the Constitution not only to enable a multiplicity of political, economic, regional, and religious beliefs to exist but also to promote their expansion in number. The motto *E pluribus unum*—out of many, one—required "the many" to retain their diverse and differing characteristics but also to respect community-held values. As Thomas Jefferson said, arguing for freedom of religions, "Divided we stand."

The United States would lock itself into a national identity defined by diversity through waves of demographic diversification, notably in the major flows of immigration of 1880–1924 and in the mid-twentieth century, the latter opening the United States to immigration from all over the world, making America the first, and still the only, global nation.

Alexis de Tocqueville's *Democracy in America* has as its main theme the question of whether democracy can be made to work in America by finding a balance between liberty and equality and in governing diversity. Tocqueville notably concluded that America was unique in that only here were religion and liberty compatible; elsewhere, he said, religion always tries to constrict freedom of choice and liberty always tries to struggle against religious dominance. But in America, Tocqueville said, pointing to the country's "point of departure" in the early colonists of New England, religion saw liberty as the arena for its practice and liberty saw religion as the cradle of its growth—as when the Puritan congregation was transformed into the New England town meeting.

Tocqueville deliberately did not cover the South, as he saw the slave economy as a system that could not be governed by the United States. In 1903, W. E. B. DuBois published *The Souls of Black Folk*, which in a way completed what Tocqueville had left out and offered thoughts about the United States as a whole, with black-white diversity compatible with a democracy.

Much of the United States' history has been burdened with slavery and its legacy. The ideal in the Declaration of Independence, "All men are created equal," was simply incompatible with slavery. With magnificent leadership from President Lincoln and through a searing Civil War, the Union was held together and slavery was abolished, but the renunciation of slavery did not end racial discrimination. Only a few decades ago, widespread demonstrations involving race galvanized many cities, including the nation's capital, and racial tensions continue to plague American society. I described some of my own experiences in previous chapters: striving to find jobs and welcoming neighborhoods for black workers, helping in the desegregation of Southern schools.

With due recognition of continuing problems in the United States, it is also true that great progress has been made, and not only recently. By the early twentieth century, and quite clearly during the course of World War II, the United States was getting better at managing diversity. The "melting pot" idea contributed to this. In the middle of the twentieth century, the US military was desegregated. By now, we have had two black secretaries of state and a re-elected black president, two black attorneys general, and a black chairman of the Joint Chiefs of Staff.

Perhaps Martin Luther King Jr.'s "I Have a Dream" speech can provide the thought as well as the inspiration we need. The speech belongs among the fundamental documents about the meaning of America. King affirmed the founders' vision, calling their writings "a promissory note" and refuting the critics who criticized the founders as no more than slaveholders and propertied special interests. In the end King stressed that tolerance is not enough: we must move beyond tolerance to brotherhood. He echoed Washington's call for a virtuous people by saying that blacks should be judged by "the content of their character." It remains a major statement on governing diversity.

History Repeats

THE WORLD is facing new strategic problems, which can be expected to put new strains on the skills of statecraft. But even the "strategic earthquake" that is rattling patterns of government and the relationships among states builds upon familiar, though intensified, patterns.

Let's review the way to think about foreign and security policy, and how to develop strategy.

First, take steps to assure and show the world that we can achieve what we set out to achieve, that a capacity to execute is always on display.

Second, be realistic. Throw away your rose-colored glasses. See the world as it is. That doesn't mean seeing only bad things. Don't be afraid to recognize an opportunity when it comes along.

Third, be strong. Of course, that means military strength; but economic strength is essential to a strong military. But we also need to have self-confidence and strength of purpose in our country.

Fourth, develop a US agenda. What is it that we want to achieve? Be careful not to think initially about the other guy's agenda and adjust to it—or you will be negotiating with yourself.

Then be ready to engage, but be clear: no empty threats. This boot-camp wisdom, often ignored, is essential wisdom.

The implication of these rules is that strength and diplomacy are not alternatives but rather are complementary to each other. As I mentioned earlier, diplomacy without strength is a loser; strength without diplomacy can erode because it can lose meaning.

The world today seems almost suddenly awash in change. Economies struggle everywhere, the Middle East is in flames, and borders seem to mean less than ever before. The proliferation of, and the rising possibility of the use of, nuclear weapons threaten all mankind. There are potentially severe consequences of a warming climate.

There is a virtually global effort opposed to the long-standing state system for bringing order to the world. And there are more refugees today than at any time since the end of World War II. All this is in sharp contrast to the economic and security commons that coalesced as the Cold War came to an end.

Today's turmoil is increasingly driven by *horizontal* loyalties: that is, the Marxist-Leninist view that an industrial worker in Marseilles has greater solidarity with an industrial worker in Yokohama than either does with his people or his nation. This horizontal ideological solidarity has manifested itself before. Today it has the potential of being sharpened into a revolution against the established border-defined order of states, as is occurring most vividly in the Middle East.

This strategic earthquake represents an accelerating decline in the management of the international state system. Many of the states that constitute the system struggle with their own problems of governance; at the same time, the system, after a long increase in mutual obligations and interactions, is under deadly attack from outside enemies who are pledged to destroy and replace it. The state system depends upon respect for the borders of countries, but borders are being softened or even erased. Most visible are the actions of Vladimir Putin's Russia. He attacked Georgia in 2008 and wound up carving out two new countries: Abkhazia and South Ossetia. More recently, and partly as a response to the movement of Ukraine in the direction of European rule of law and greater interaction with Western European countries, he seized Crimea and is in the process of trying to erase the borders of eastern Ukraine. Russian arms have been fired to shoot down a civilian passenger aircraft. Putin is surely playing a very weak hand and that weakness is beginning to show, but he plays that hand very aggressively.

Meanwhile, in Western Europe, leaders are gradually reducing the meaning of borders as they seek to homogenize into "Europe" all the ancient cultures of that region (and not just its currencies). The stresses produced by this effort are all too evident as the dispersion of sovereign powers leaves a sense of uncertainty and indecisiveness in the region amid continuing economic problems.

The Arab regimes, at least since the post–Second World War period, had been telling the world that all was well in the Middle East except for one thing: the existence of Israel. American administrations across the years generally accepted this narrative and devoted their efforts to attempts to resolve the Arab-Israeli conflict.

At the same time, the Arab regimes, starting in the mid-1970s, recognized the growing existence of a horizontal, religiously radical political ideology that held a dangerous potential for the regimes themselves. The regimes therefore began in various ways to try to co-opt the Islamists by subsidizing them and urging them to redirect their threats away from the regimes and toward Israel and European and American targets.

The overthrow of rulers in Tunisia and Egypt and of Saddam Hussein's regime in Iraq caused the Islamists to envision overthrowing other Arab regimes. This meant that the old narrative—the only Middle East problem was Israel—was no longer plausible or sustainable; it was now a Muslim-on-Muslim conflict with nothing to do with Israel. And within this contest re-emerged the centuries-old mutual hatred of Sunni and Shia.

These layers of intra-Muslim conflict have coalesced into one, ever-larger civil war between the state regimes inside the international state system and the Islamist ideologues who would overthrow them and take the entire region out of the international system and into their religiously driven new world order.

Even so, the ideology of jihadist terror groups like ISIS is not new under the sun. Consider this passage from *Thomas Jefferson and the Tripoli Pirates: The Forgotten War that Changed American History*, in which Brian Kilmeade and Don Yaeger wrote about America's early clash with the Barbary pirates. In 1786, when John Adams was ambassador to London and Thomas Jefferson to Paris, Adams invited Jefferson to talk with Tripoli's ambassador in London, Sidi Haji Abdrahaman. After a frustrating effort to negotiate,

> Adams asked how the Barbary states could justify "[making] war upon nations who had done them no injury."
>
> According to the holy book, the Qur'an, Abdrahaman explained, "all nations which had not acknowledged the Prophet were sinners, whom it was the right and duty of the faithful to plunder and enslave." . . .
>
> "Every mussulman," he explained, "who was slain in this warfare was sure to go to paradise." . . . In his culture, the takers of ships, the enslavers of men, the Barbarians who extorted bribes for safe passage, were all justified by the teaching of the prophet Muhammad. "It was written in our Qur'an," he said simply.

After he became president, Jefferson confronted the Barbary powers with military force. We could use a little of his wisdom and strength today.

Ever since the time of the French Revolution, statesmen and scholars have been aware that the danger coming from the "horizontal" threat reaches a climax when the ideology acquires a territorial foothold and becomes an armed doctrine fielding an army. In the summer of 2014 the world witnessed the sudden emergence of ISIS and its self-proclaimed Islamic State and Caliphate. ISIS's goal was never in doubt, as one fighter said: "We are opposed to countries," that is, to the world of states.

Another dimension of threat comes into play: religion. From 1648 to the mid-1990s, religion was thought to have been neutralized as a cause of conflict in international affairs. During the premodern period, religion was largely hostile to diversity, demanding that all peoples under its purview adhere to a single way of belief and practice. The modern age sought to neutralize this tendency, declaring that while each state could practice the religions of its choice, religious doctrines and scriptures should be kept out of interstate negotiations, a precept that worked well for a long time.

However, radical Islamism finds it intolerable to cooperate with unbelievers. After three centuries in which religion was kept out of international affairs, the rise of radical Islam has posed a severe setback to the cause of governing diversity.

Added to this growing font of instability, we see a burst of technology producing a variety of small, smart, and cheap weapons and putting deadly power in the hands of individuals, small dissident groups, and larger entities. Meanwhile, the American grand strategy seems, to countries around the world, to consist of withdrawal.

Is there a wise response to this strategic earthquake? Yes.

We begin with the US military. Our armed forces clearly need support for their force structure, training, the acquisition of weapons, and, even more important, the costly effort to develop weapons of the future. But the military budget is threatened by swelling health care and pension commitments. Those commitments, if not reined in, will crowd out the basic functions of the military. The same medicine must be applied to federal entitlements more generally.

We need energy security. Russia is attempting to build and extend a sphere of influence beyond its borders. One of its strengths is the dependence of many countries, particularly in Eastern Europe and the Baltic states, on Moscow for supplies of oil and gas. Russia is willing to cut off such supplies in the middle of winter to get what it wants. The first step to counter this threat is a European energy initiative. The United States has recently developed the ability to produce oil and gas far beyond supplies of earlier times, and we have lifted export controls. We should develop liquefied natural gas facilities and encourage the use of the new energy-production tools in European countries that have potential capacity. Thus we could ensure enough capacity in every nation to sharply weaken Russia's threat to cut off supplies.

We must guarantee that our military capabilities, in harmony with NATO, are strong and properly distributed to face future threats.

And then there is the situation in Ukraine. Ukraine's armed forces need training and equipment. More basically, Ukraine must lessen the corruption in its governmental processes and take advantage of its natural capabilities to get its economy moving in a positive direction.

If we are able to put these policies in place, Russia will see that it is not walking into a vacuum but into a stone wall. Russia is playing such a weak hand—economically and demographically—that we also must be ready to engage with Russia, expecting that at some point along the way Russia will see the advantages of working within a collaborative state system.

But now Russia has returned to the Middle East in collaboration with Iran, first in support of Bashar Assad's Syrian regime, but, no doubt, in a combined effort to extend Iranian reach throughout the Middle East as sanctions are lifted and Iran's resources are strongly increased.

The Middle East and ISIS present difficult and complex issues, alongside the growing scourge of international terrorism, but certain paths come into focus. We saw more than our share of terrorism during the Reagan years, and I became a hawk on the subject. At the time, our prevailing policy was essentially one of law enforcement: if a crime was committed, we would find the culprit, try him, and punish him. In my 1984 speech I changed the subject, arguing that the better course of action was to beef up intelligence, find out what was going to happen before it happened, and then take preventive action. This was a sharp shift in attitude; fortunately, President Reagan agreed. (This argument, still very timely, is found in the appendix to this book.)

We must do everything we can to limit Islamist terror groups' military and financial capabilities. Initially this means a strong diplomatic effort to persuade Arab states that have a record of trying to buy off ISIS that that tactic is self-defeating. Air power can greatly restrict Islamist groups' access to oil supplies, as can denying them access to markets.

Our rules of engagement must not allow civilian presence to provide a privileged sanctuary so as to shield offensive military weapons.

The United States also must develop an effective regional force for the Middle East. One unusual potential coalition would comprise forces from Saudi Arabia, Jordan, Egypt, and Israel, plus Iraqi Kurds and others, perhaps Turkey, with help from traditional European allies.

Once ISIS experiences a sharp decline in military success, its appeal will decline. Nevertheless, we also need to seek ways to understand that appeal and deal effectively with it. Every country in the West, not to mention Russia and China, needs to be on guard against potential terrorist threats that may spring from the Islamist group's carcass.

China is not to be ignored. A constructive relationship with China is essential to American foreign policy. Strains are evident, but creative and resourceful diplomacy can deal with them. Here is some common-sense advice for improving that relationship.

Leaders of the two countries—alternatively, their authorized secretaries of state, defense, and treasury—should list all areas where cooperation and interaction benefit each country. The list will be fairly long, but it will be dominated by the economic advantages to both countries of their broad economic interaction. Other obvious areas of collaboration include terrorism, climate change, and nuclear proliferation.

China's competing claims with Japan over the Senkaku Islands lay dormant for a long while, as both sides simply agreed to disagree. Skillful diplomacy should be able to put the issue back to sleep. The South China Sea presents more difficult issues, but perhaps there is a template that could be used. A careful joint study by a council of all the countries with interacting borders, including sea borders, with a rotating chairmanship can spell out and respect the rules. Such an approach has been used to handle issues in the Arctic, so perhaps the

Arctic Council can serve as a template. In the meantime, we must sail and fly in the area to maintain freedom of the seas in this vital region.

China and the United States have a shared stake in taking every possible step to get better control of nuclear weapons. They could lead others in a joint enterprise of countries working on this issue. President Obama has been pursuing ways to get better control of fissile material; perhaps this could be the stimulus for a global nuclear control enterprise.

Progress also is being made in verification. Traditional technical means remain available. A template of on-site inspection in the most recent START treaty between the United States and Russia presents a working arrangement that other structures could build upon.

Better information and communication everywhere are increasingly making the world an open book. In this world, to sound a familiar theme, we must garden. Any gardener knows that if you plant something, wander off, and then come back six months later, all you have is weeds. So you learn to keep at it.

The same is true in diplomacy. Listen to people, talk to people, and discuss possibilities, problems, and opportunities. Get to know others and build a relationship of trust. Then, when problems arise, you have a basis for work in a constructive way. A patient gardener will always be rewarded with good fruit.

Governance: Family, Community, and Beyond

GOVERNANCE IS ESSENTIAL; human society will collapse without it. The need is perpetual and the conduct of it is hard. Recent events have made governance even harder as we recognize a world in ever-widening disorder. How should we deal with this? From experience and from the bottom up.

Is there one major theme or challenge that, if we grasp it, can shape a coherent, comprehensive approach to governance in a disordered world? Yes. From the dawn of time, the fundamental quest has been for ways to reconcile the reality of human diversity and governance. At the same time, there has been a quest for a sense of unity that the widest array of diverse groups can support—while maintaining their own distinctive character.

"A vision to dizzy and appal" is how Cardinal John Henry Newman described the sweep of the world in a striking passage in 1864. The vision Newman described is even more disorienting today because powerful centrifugal and centripetal forces are at work at the same time, pulling and pushing each diverse entity to either fall apart or submit to some centralizing demand.

At every level of human organization throughout history, we see a purposive design for governing diversity. And if any one level breaks down or begins to worsen rather than solve the problems of human cooperation, all other levels will feel the harm and accordingly will be weakened.

Timothy Garton Ash, a Hoover colleague, describes the organizing process in his book *Freedom in Diversity,* touching on matters such as citizenship, education, work opportunities, and appropriate governance. In my own somewhat similar view, the family is the fundamental unit of governance.

The family generates diversity; its members are not alike, yet they share a fundamental bond. Parents who want their children to be just like them invariably cannot make them so. The family is the first example of the importance of *E pluribus unum*. It is an ancient insight that the household is the first human political and economic unit. What is the bond that holds them together in all their diversity and without invidious regard to talents or objective merit? It is something more than genetic-biologic connection. When asked what a family is, Robert Frost said, "When you go there, they have to take you in." You know there is a place you belong, where you have a sense of ownership and responsibility.

The significance of marriage for governing diversity has been a major part of the rise of civilization but has not been clearly understood in our day. In the modern era, each marriage created a distinct, diverse entity and a new family was created independent of tribes. This did much to diminish and eventually condemn the pre-civilizational phenomenon of blood feuds between clans. Of course, in many parts of the world this still has not been crossed. One of the main causes of social tension in the Middle East today is the desire of young people to escape tribal domination and emerge as "modern" in marriage and independent lives. In the United States, the breakdown or fracturing of the family and marriage has been documented for close to fifty years. We have a problem!

Next comes community. Not since the primitive or pioneer subsistence household have families lived in isolation, and those who have done so have sought to emerge from that situation as quickly as possible. Communities—villages, towns, and cities—are necessary to promote and take advantage of diversity. Economically and socially, diversity enhances productivity, as a community needs farmers, grocers, merchants, doctors, police and firefighters, and so on. The size of the market will determine the extent of diversity. And because people of differing interests will choose different forms of employment and, consequently, those different kinds of jobs will reinforce different and often competing interests, governance becomes an imperative to administer justice and ensure individual rights.

Community diversity is a well of strength. The small town was, for two hundred or more years, the backbone of American character and an exemplar of the importance of faith. The American small town, it is not too much to say, provided the soldiers, sailors, Marines, and aviators who won the Second World War; they had a distinctive diversity of skills and displayed a common purpose and patriotism. American cities in the first half of the twentieth century thrived because of ethnically diverse neighborhoods and their manufacturing and marketing jobs.

Some of our communities, large and small, have lost their vibrant diversity. Resources and regulations now distort how they operate and how they see themselves. A natural compatibility between diversity and governance has been lost and must somehow be regained.

The company is the third level of organization. The American company or corporation (or foundation, association, society, organization to produce usable goods) can be understood as "civil society," the layer of human collective action and interaction that exists, and thrives, by contributing economic well-being and creating a sense of belonging. This layer is by definition an arena for boundless diversity. Tocqueville wrote that such associations were the most essential part of American democracy. Companies are as diverse as human needs and desires themselves, and to meet such expectations, companies come and go, grow or wither, with new and ever more diverse types in evidence. And companies themselves are internally diverse, starting with labor-management relations. They are perpetually engaged in an effort to find a productive and profitable outcome through attention to, and integration of, diverse operations: supply chains, vertical integration, quality control, time to market, engineering, invention, competition, compensation, and human resources. They balance and harmonize short-term results and a distant horizon.

If you add up family, community, and company, you have a sense of belonging, ownership, and the ability to participate. The result is civic responsibility.

It is immensely significant that during the Cold War the ideology of the communist countries outlawed civil society precisely *because* it was diverse: the party rulers wanted no layer to exist between the state and the person. They wanted to keep the individual naked and powerless under the direction of the regime. After the Cold War, the greatest problem for newly free lands in Eastern Europe was how to re-establish civil society and private companies as a layer of diversity.

The most consequential shift in the structure of international affairs in the past century may be the decline of the concept of the nation-state—one state made up of one nationality—and the emergence of the multiethnic, multicultural, multinational state. In the latter category, only the United States has politically, morally, and culturally been reasonably comfortable and reasonably successful. Increasing numbers of states such as France, Brazil, and Japan have been struggling with the concept.

The Cold War's end terminated the totalitarian dimension of ideological rule. In China, however, the Communist Party has grown ever more determined to retain and advance a single form of mentality and political adherence to party doctrine. Diversity of opinion is permitted but only up to a point, and is under threat wherever such opinions challenge the party line. Religion, which has seen an upsurge in China, is especially worrisome to Chinese officials.

By contrast, some parts of the world understood diversity a long time ago. I recall a lesson I learned from a man with a deep understanding of this civic value.

During my first trip to Israel in 1969, I was fortunate to be taken in by the engaging, iconic mayor of Jerusalem, Teddy Kollek. On my first evening, we went from party to party, where everyone was having a good time. After a while, Kollek took me to his office and I realized that he was teaching me something.

Kollek said, "My job as mayor is to make Jerusalem a beautiful picture, but it is not a traditional painting in which colors merge. My Jerusalem is a mosaic. You've seen these groups this evening. They aren't just Jews and Arabs, but there are distinctive groups of Jews and distinctive groups of Arabs. My job is to see that they can retain their distinctive characteristics as long as they don't infringe on the ability of others to retain theirs. And then, of course, I want them all to be content—to live under the Golden Dome of Jerusalem. That's my beautiful picture: a mosaic."

Teddy Kollek recognized that Jerusalem was a diverse city and, because he understood profoundly what that meant, he was able to keep this mosaic in place for quite a long while. Most people think he was a genius at governance. He is desperately needed now.

Teddy's theme of coherence is absent from most of the world's power centers. Europe, Russia, the Middle East, China, India, and even the United States show signs of some form of identity crisis. When national identity is uncertain, nationalism rises, and nationalism produces fragmentation and mutual antagonism. Diversity proliferates without the bond of substantive meaning.

There is a final, large, organizing principle: the region. While the state has succeeded the empire as the basic unit of world affairs in the modern era (although empires have never given up trying to reverse that success), the region remains a natural entity for international action and/or cooperation. The United Nations Charter specifically recognizes the value of "regional organizations and associations." These provide some manner of consensus-based regional commonality of governance while respecting the diversity of language, culture, and political systems of the states within a region.

The regional concept has never quite lived up its potential. The Organization of American States had high aspirations but did not make much of them. The Organization of African Unity has never found the unity it was created to attain. Only the Association of Southeast Asian Nations (ASEAN) has been successful, not only in finding a governance-diversity role for its region but also in getting the respect and careful involvement of out-of-region state partners. ASEAN is now taking action to make itself into a free-trade zone.

Regional identities are vulnerable to certain problems. The notion of regional associations may degrade to the old idea of "spheres of influence," a dangerous form that the United Nations, for one, was designed to prevent. World War II was essentially fought over this issue: imperial Japan sought to impose by force a Tokyo-dominated "Greater East Asia Co-Prosperity Sphere" and Nazi Germany tried to conquer Europe from the Atlantic to the Urals to secure *Lebensraum*, a vastly expanded sphere of influence for the German people. Both of these powers were driven by a racist ideology, which of course is the antithesis of an acceptance of human diversity.

Should spheres of influence return, it would be a deadly blow to the universality of "the doctrine of the equality of states," a profound doctrine that ensures that each individual state, in some juridical sense, is equal to any other state. This is a concept at the heart of the task of governing diversity and one that is at the heart of the design of the United Nations, where the General Assembly gives every state one vote as equals while, at the same time, placing governance—at least theoretically—over international security in the UN Security Council, a recognition of the reality of the world's great powers and the concept of the balance of power. The concept of spheres of influence would discard all this as each sphere would be directed by dictation by the strongest power in the region in a return to "might makes right." There are signs that China is moving in this direction with regard to all the maritime waters of East and Southeast Asia and that Russia has similar ambitions toward Ukraine and the Baltics as well as other territories formerly controlled by Moscow in the days of the USSR. In the Middle East at present, there is a war over which Muslim power will rule the region as a sphere of influence.

The alternative to this deleterious scenario can be found in the shaping of North America as a new kind of regional association, one which may adopt the positive aspects of ASEAN even while improving on some of the drawbacks of the UN's idea of regional organization. There is no bureaucracy managing the fast-emerging region of North America. Trade contains a significant proportion of value of the importing country. Each country's sovereign control of such key economic matters as monetary and fiscal policy is maintained. People and organizations are simply responding to incentives. A few similar ideas can be heard to be under consideration, one being that of an "Intermarium" association of Eastern European states in a north-south belt from the Baltic to the Black Sea or Mediterranean, an association that could resist the encroachment of Russia and perhaps avoid the fecklessness of the European Union as an experiment in governing diversity.

A Time to Trust, to Lead, and to Hope

I REMAIN a genuine optimist even though we seem surrounded by difficult problems and are not at the top of our game.

I continue to be inspired by individuals such as George Washington, who, in his Farewell Address and other work, recognized that the United States was going to be the world's first-ever free country. Freedom always carries the seeds of danger; it can be turned into a license for self-serving, self-indulgent behavior of a sort that could lead to near-anarchy and destroy freedom. So a free country, Washington knew, requires a virtuous people, people with families living in good communities, people who understand that just because something is permitted, or lawful, does not mean that it should be done.

Ronald Reagan, too, will always be one of my guiding lights. His thoughts and statements tie together all the levels of community, from the individual and family to the family of nations. He spoke tellingly about the difference between the nation-state and the multi-ethnic, multicultural, multireligion state when he noted that a man had written to him saying, "You can go to live in France, but you cannot become a Frenchman. You can go to live in Germany or Turkey or Japan, but you cannot become a German, a Turk, or . . . Japanese. But anyone, from any corner of the Earth, can come to live in America and become an American."

Reagan was famous for the importance he put on trust—"trust but verify"—which holds true at all levels and recognizes that a willingness to verify promotes trust. Above all, governing diversity requires trust *among all*. Without trust, regulations to impose standards of conduct proliferate. Regulations become laws and the laws proliferate too, bringing more and more litigation, which only keeps diverse peoples apart and obstructs the goal of *E pluribus unum*.

We can unite citizens under sound principles and mechanisms. Here we remember the Bill of Rights, with its guarantee that the rights of a minority cannot be taken away by the majority. Proceduralism extends such safeguards. If the subcultures of a state follow the set of procedures required by the state—paying taxes, for example, or accepting military service—then they should be free to follow whatever substantive beliefs in practice they consider essential. (This is the way the international state system itself is designed to work.)

We must address law and morality in a way that approaches consensus that they are not the same thing. That is, the law of the state should not be extended to attempt to define and regulate all morality. Governmental attempts to limit pluralism are self-defeating. The willingness, indeed commitment, by government to welcome pluralism—the more diversity the better—has served the interests of the diverse groups even as it ensures that no one of them will rise to domination over others or over the state itself. This applies to both religious and political pluralism. Religions that are dogmatically "uniate," that is, that cannot bring themselves to share the public space with other religions, may simply be incompatible with the very concept of governing diversity. Clearly the new phenomenon of the Islamist State and Caliphate fails this test.

The United States must take a leading role if the international state system—the structure for world order in general—is to survive growing disarray and danger. Our task will be to support, shore up, and defend the legitimate states of the international system and to oppose their enemies.

At the same time, the international state system has to demand *more* of a state: at heart, equal justice under law for all peoples within the state. From now on, the legitimacy of a state should depend upon whether it governs rather than represses diversity.

I know, but more important, I *realize*, as a result of a great variety of experiences that we can pursue these aims at home and abroad, rekindle economic expansion, get our government back to a pattern of accomplishment, and revive our leadership on the world stage. With our determined and competent leadership, others will follow.

The Cold War has ended. People almost everywhere live longer and are healthier than ever; the world's improved quality of life can underpin stability and progress. As before, leadership is not domination. But when the United States comes to the table with ideas and a willingness to work on the problem, constructive results have always emerged.

From a personal standpoint, I had the experience of watching President Reagan transform our country and our surroundings in a most impressive way. When he took office, inflation was high, the economy was going nowhere, our spirits were down, the Soviet Union was in Afghanistan, and the Cold War was as cold as it could get. When he left office, inflation was under control, the economy was moving well, we had regained our self-confidence, and the Cold War was all over except for the shouting.

We, with our friends and allies, hold a winning hand. We simply need to play that hand with skill and enthusiasm.

Appendix

Terrorism and the Modern World

Secretary of State George P. Shultz
October 25, 1984

*The following is an address by Secretary Shultz before the Park
Avenue Synagogue, New York, October 25, 1984.*

Someday terrorism will no longer be a timely subject for a speech,
but that day has not arrived. Less than two weeks ago, one of the
oldest and greatest nations of the Western world almost lost its prime
minister, Margaret Thatcher, to the modern barbarism that we call
terrorism. A month ago, the American Embassy annex in East Beirut
was nearly destroyed by a terrorist truck bomb, the third major attack
on Americans in Lebanon within the past two years. To list all the
other acts of brutality that terrorists have visited upon civilized society in recent years would be impossible here because that list is too
long. It is too long to name and too long to tolerate.

But I am here to talk about terrorism as a phenomenon in our
modern world—about what terrorism is and what it is not. We have
learned a great deal about terrorism in recent years. We have learned
much about the terrorists themselves, their supporters, their diverse
methods, their underlying motives, and their eventual goals. What

once may have seemed the random, senseless, violent acts of a few crazed individuals has come into clearer focus. A pattern of terrorist violence has emerged. It is an alarming pattern, but it is something that we can identify and, therefore, a threat that we can devise concrete measures to combat. The knowledge we have accumulated about terrorism over the years can provide the basis for a coherent strategy to deal with the phenomenon, if we have the will to turn our understanding into action.

The Meaning of Terrorism

We have learned that terrorism is, above all, a form of political violence. It is neither random nor without purpose. Today, we are confronted with a wide assortment of terrorist groups which, alone or in concert, orchestrate acts of violence to achieve distinctly political ends. Their stated objectives may range from separatist causes to revenge for ethnic grievances to social and political revolution. Their methods may be just as diverse: from planting homemade explosives in public places to suicide car bombings to kidnappings and political assassinations. But the overarching goal of all terrorists is the same: they are trying to impose their will by force—a special kind of force designed to create an atmosphere of fear. The horrors they inflict are not simply a new manifestation of traditional social conflict; they are depraved opponents of civilization itself, aided by the technology of modern weaponry. The terrorists want people to feel helpless and defenseless; they want people to lose faith in their government's capacity to protect them and thereby to undermine the legitimacy of the government itself, or its policies, or both.

The terrorists profit from the anarchy caused by their violence. They succeed when governments change their policies out of intimidation. But the terrorist can even be satisfied if a government responds to terror by clamping down on individual rights and freedoms. Governments that overreact, even in self-defense, may only undermine their own legitimacy, as they unwittingly serve the terrorists' goals. The terrorist succeeds if a government responds to violence with repressive, polarizing behavior that alienates the government from the people.

The Threat to Democracy

We must understand, however, that terrorism, wherever it takes place, is directed in an important sense against us, the democracies—against our most basic values and often our fundamental strategic interests. Because terrorism relies on brutal violence as its only tool, it will always be the enemy of democracy. For democracy rejects the indiscriminate or improper use of force and relies instead on the peaceful settlement of disputes through legitimate political processes.

The moral bases of democracy—the principles of individual rights, freedom of thought and expression, freedom of religion—are powerful barriers against those who seek to impose their will, their ideologies, or their religious beliefs by force. Whether in Israel or Lebanon or Turkey or Italy or West Germany or Northern Ireland, a terrorist has no patience for the orderly processes of democratic society and, therefore, he seeks to destroy it. Indeed, terrorism seeks to destroy what all of us here are seeking to build.

The United States and the other democracies are morally committed to certain ideals and to a humane vision of the future. Nor is our vision limited to within our borders. In our foreign policies, as well, we try to foster the kind of world that promotes peaceful settlement of disputes, one that welcomes beneficial change. We do not practice terrorism, and we seek to build a world which holds no place for terrorist violence, a world in which human rights are respected by all governments, a world based on the rule of law.

And there is yet another reason why we are attacked. If freedom and democracy are the targets of terrorism, it is clear that totalitarianism is its ally. The number of terrorist incidents in totalitarian states is minimal, and those against their personnel abroad are markedly fewer than against the West. And this is not only because police states offer less room for terrorists to carry out acts of violence. States that support and sponsor terrorist actions have managed in recent years to co-opt and manipulate the terrorist phenomenon in pursuit of their own strategic goals.

It is not a coincidence that most acts of terrorism occur in areas of importance to the West. More than 80 percent of the world's terrorist attacks in 1983 occurred in Western Europe, Latin America, and the Middle East. Terrorism in this context is not just criminal activity but an unbridled form of warfare.

Today, international links among terrorist groups are more clearly understood. And Soviet and Soviet-bloc support is also more clearly understood. We face a diverse family of dangers. Iran and the Soviet Union are hardly allies, but they both share a fundamental hostility to the West. When Libya and the PLO [Palestine Liberation Organization] provide arms and training to the communists in Central America, they are aiding Soviet-supported Cuban efforts to undermine our security in that vital region. When the Red Brigades in Italy and the Red Army Faction in Germany assault free countries in the name of communist ideology, they hope to shake the West's self-confidence, unity, and will to resist intimidation. The terrorists who assault Israel—and, indeed, the Marxist Provisional IRA [Irish Republican Army] in Northern Ireland—are ideological enemies of the United States. We cannot and we will not succumb to the likes of Khomeini and Gadhafi.

We also now see a close connection between terrorism and international narcotics trafficking. Cuba and Nicaragua, in particular, have used narcotics smugglers to funnel guns and money to terrorists and insurgents in Colombia. Other communist countries, like Bulgaria, have also been part of the growing link between drugs and terrorism.

We should understand the Soviet role in international terrorism without exaggeration or distortion. One does not have to believe that the Soviets are puppeteers and the terrorists marionettes; violent or fanatic individuals and groups can exist in almost any society.

But in many countries, terrorism would long since have withered away had it not been for significant support from outside. When Israel went into Lebanon in 1982, Israeli forces uncovered irrefutable evidence that the Soviet Union had been arming and training the PLO and other groups. Today, there is no reason to think that Soviet support for terrorist groups around the world has diminished. Here, as elsewhere, there is a wide gap between Soviet words and Soviet deeds, a gap that is very clear, for instance, when you put Soviet support for terrorist groups up against the empty rhetoric of the resolution against so-called "state terrorism" which the USSR has submitted to this year's UN General Assembly. The Soviets condemn terrorism, but in practice they connive with terrorist groups when they think it serves their own purposes, and their goal is always the same: to weaken liberal democracy and undermine world stability.

The Moral and Strategic Stakes

The stakes in our war against terrorism, therefore, are high. We have already seen the horrible cost in innocent lives that terrorist violence has incurred. But perhaps even more horrible is the damage that terrorism threatens to wreak on our modern civilization. For centuries mankind has strived to build a world in which the highest human aspirations can be fulfilled.

We have pulled ourselves out of a state of barbarism and removed the affronts to human freedom and dignity that are inherent to that condition. We have sought to free ourselves from that primitive existence described by Hobbes where life is lived in "continual fear and danger of violent death . . . nasty, brutish, and short." We have sought to create, instead, a world where universal respect for human rights and democratic values makes a better life possible. We in the democracies can attest to all that man is capable of achieving if he renounces violence and brute force, if he is free to think, write, vote, and worship as he pleases. Yet all of these hard-won gains are threatened by terrorism.

Terrorism is a step backward; it is a step toward anarchy and decay. In the broadest sense, terrorism represents a return to barbarism in the modern age. If the modern world cannot face up to the challenge, then terrorism, and the lawlessness and inhumanity that come with it, will gradually undermine all that the modern world has achieved and make further progress impossible.

Obstacles to Meeting the Challenge

The magnitude of the threat posed by terrorism is so great that we cannot afford to confront it with half-hearted and poorly organized measures. Terrorism is a contagious disease that will inevitably spread if it goes untreated. We need a strategy to cope with terrorism in all of its varied manifestations. We need to summon the necessary resources and determination to fight it and, with international cooperation, eventually stamp it out. And we have to recognize that the burden falls on us, the democracies—no one else will cure the disease for us.

Yet clearly we face obstacles, some of which arise precisely because we are democracies. The nature of the terrorist assault is, in many ways, alien to us. Democracies like to act on the basis of known facts and shared knowledge. Terrorism is clandestine and mysterious by nature. Terrorists rely on secrecy, and, therefore, it is hard to know for certain who has committed an atrocity.

Democracies also rely on reason and persuasive logic to make decisions. It is hard for us to understand the fanaticism and apparent irrationality of many terrorists, especially those who kill and commit suicide in the belief that they will be rewarded in the afterlife. The psychopathic ruthlessness and brutality of terrorism is an aberration in our culture and alien to our heritage.

And it is an unfortunate irony that the very qualities that make democracies so hateful to the terrorists—our respect for the rights and freedoms of the individual—also make us particularly vulnerable. Precisely because we maintain the most open societies, terrorists have unparalleled opportunity to strike at us. Terrorists seek to make democracies embattled and afraid, to break down democratic accountability, due process, and order; they hope we will turn toward repression or succumb to chaos.

These are the challenges we must live with. We will certainly not alter the democratic values that we so cherish in order to fight terrorism. We will have to find ways to fight back without undermining everything we stand for.

Combating Moral Confusion

There is another obstacle that we have created for ourselves that we should overcome—that we must overcome—if we are to fight terrorism effectively. The obstacle I am referring to is confusion.

We cannot begin to address this monumental challenge to decent civilized society until we clear our heads of the confusion about terrorism, in many ways the *moral* confusion, that still seems to plague us. Confusion can lead to paralysis, and it is a luxury that we simply cannot afford.

The confusion about terrorism has taken many forms. In recent years, we have heard some ridiculous distortions even about what the word "terrorism" means. The idea, for instance, that denying food stamps to some is a form of terrorism cannot be entertained by serious people. And those who would argue, as recently some in Great Britain have, that physical violence by strikers can be equated with "the violence of unemployment" are, in the words of *The Economist,* "a menace to democracy everywhere." In a real democracy, violence is unequivocally bad. Such distortions are dangerous, because words are important. When we distort our language, we may distort our thinking, and we hamper our efforts to find solutions to the grave problems we face.

There has been, however, a more serious kind of confusion surrounding the issue of terrorism: the confusion between the terrorist act itself and the political goals that the terrorists claim to seek.

The grievances that terrorists supposedly seek to redress through acts of violence may or may not be legitimate. The terrorist acts themselves, however, can never be legitimate. And legitimate causes can never justify or excuse terrorism. Terrorist means discredit their ends.

We have all heard the insidious claim that "one man's terrorist is another man's freedom fighter." When I spoke on the subject of terrorism this past June, I quoted the powerful rebuttal to this kind of moral relativism made by the late Senator Henry Jackson. His statement bears repeating today: "The idea that one person's 'terrorist' is another's 'freedom fighter,'" he said, "cannot be sanctioned. Freedom fighters or revolutionaries don't blow up buses containing non-combatants; terrorist murderers do. Freedom fighters don't set out to capture and slaughter schoolchildren; terrorist murderers do. Freedom fighters don't assassinate innocent businessmen, or hijack and hold hostage innocent men, women, and children; terrorist murderers do. It is a disgrace that democracies would allow the treasured word 'freedom' to be associated with acts of terrorists." So spoke Scoop Jackson.

We cannot afford to let an Orwellian corruption of language obscure our understanding of terrorism. We know the difference between terrorists and freedom fighters, and as we look around the world, we have no trouble telling one from the other.

How tragic it would be if democratic societies so lost confidence in their own moral legitimacy that they lost sight of the obvious: that violence directed against democracy or the hopes for democracy lacks fundamental justification. Democracy offers the opportunity for peaceful change, legitimate political competition, and redress of grievances. We must oppose terrorists no matter what banner they may fly. For terrorism in *any* cause is the enemy of freedom.

And we must not fall into the deadly trap of giving justification to the unacceptable acts of terrorists by acknowledging the worthy-sounding motives they may claim. Organizations such as the Provisional IRA, for instance, play on popular grievances and political and religious emotions to disguise their deadly purpose. They find ways to work through local political and religious leaders to enlist support for their brutal actions. As a result, we even find Americans contributing, we hope unwittingly, to an organization which has killed—in cold blood and without the slightest remorse—hundreds of innocent men, women, and children in Great Britain and Ireland; an organization which has assassinated senior officials and tried to assassinate the British prime minister and her entire cabinet; a professed Marxist organization which also gets support from Libya's Gadhafi and has close links with other international terrorists. The government of the United States stands firmly with the government of the United Kingdom and the government of Ireland in opposing any action that lends aid or support to the Provisional IRA.

Moral confusion about terrorism can take many forms. When two Americans and twelve Lebanese were killed at our embassy annex in East Beirut last month, for instance, we were told by some that this mass murder was an expression, albeit an extreme expression, of Arab hostility to American policy in the Middle East. We were told that this bombing happened because of a vote we cast in the United Nations, or because of our policies in Lebanon, or because of the overall state of our relations with the Arab nations, or because of our support for Israel.

We were advised by some that if we want to stop terrorism—if we want to put an end to these vicious murders—then what we need to do is change our policies. In effect, we have been told that terrorism is in some measure our own fault, and we deserved to be bombed. I can tell you here and now that the United States will not be driven off or stayed from our course or change our policy by terrorist brutality.

We cannot permit ourselves any uncertainty as to the real meaning of terrorist violence in the Middle East or anywhere else. Those who truly seek peace in the Middle East know that war and violence are no answer. Those who oppose radicalism and support negotiation are themselves the target of terrorism, whether they are Arabs or Israelis. One of the great tragedies of the Middle East, in fact, is that the many moderates on the Arab side—who are ready to live in peace with Israel—are threatened by the radicals and their terrorist henchmen and are thus stymied in their own efforts for peace.

The terrorists' principal goal in the Middle East is to destroy any progress toward a negotiated peace. And the more our policies succeed, the closer we come toward achieving our goals in the Middle East, the harder terrorists will try to stop us. The simple fact is, the terrorists are more upset about *progress* in the Middle East than they are about any alleged failures to achieve progress. Let us not forget that President Sadat [of Egypt] was murdered because he made peace, and that threats continue to be issued daily in that region because of the fear—yes, fear—that others might favor a negotiated path toward peace.

Whom would we serve by changing our policies in the Middle East in the face of the terrorist threat? Not Israel, not the moderate Arabs, not the Palestinian people, and certainly not the cause for peace. Indeed, the worst thing we could do is change our principled policies under the threat of violence. What we *must* do is support our friends and remain firm in our goals.

We have to rid ourselves of this moral confusion which lays the blame for terrorist actions on us or on our policies. We are attacked not because of what we are doing wrong but because of what we are doing right. We are right to support the security of Israel, and there is no terrorist act or threat that will change that firm determination. We are attacked not because of some mistake we are making but because of who we are and what we believe in. We must not abandon our principles, or our role in the world, or our responsibilities as the champion of freedom and peace.

The Response to Terrorism

While terrorism threatens many countries, the United States has a special responsibility. It is time for this country to make a broad national commitment to treat the challenge of terrorism with the sense of urgency and priority it deserves.

The essence of our response is simple to state: violence and aggression must be met by firm resistance. This principle holds true whether we are responding to full-scale military attacks or to the kinds of low-level conflicts that are more common in the modern world.

We are on the way to being well-prepared to deter an all-out war or a Soviet attack on our principal allies; that is why these are the least likely contingencies. It is not self-evident that we are as well-prepared and organized to deter and counter the "gray area" of intermediate challenges that we are more likely to face—the low-intensity conflict of which terrorism is a part.

We have worked hard to deter large-scale aggression by strengthening our strategic and conventional defenses, by restoring the pride and confidence of the men and women in our military, and by displaying the kind of national resolve to confront aggression that can deter potential adversaries. We have been more successful than in the past in dealing with many forms of low-level aggression. We have checked communist aggression and subversion in Central America and the Caribbean and opened the way for peaceful, democratic processes in that region. And we successfully liberated Grenada from Marxist control and returned that tiny island to freedom and self-determination.

But terrorism, which is also a form of low-level aggression, has so far posed an even more difficult challenge, for the technology of security has been outstripped by the technology of murder. And, of course, the United States is not the only nation that faces difficulties in responding to terrorism. To update President Reagan's report in the debate last Sunday, since September 1, forty-one acts of terrorism have been perpetrated by no less than fourteen terrorist groups against the people and property of twenty-one countries. Even Israel has not rid itself of the terrorist threat, despite its brave and prodigious efforts.

But no nation had more experience with terrorism than Israel, and no nation has made a greater contribution to our understanding of the problem and the best ways to confront it. By supporting organizations like the Jonathan Institute, named after the brave Israeli soldier who led and died at Entebbe, the Israeli people have helped raise international awareness of the global scope of the terrorist threat.

And Israel's contribution goes beyond the theoretical. Israel has won major battles in the war against terrorism in actions across its borders, in other continents, and in the land of Israel itself. To its great credit, the Israeli government has moved within Israel to apprehend and bring to trial its own citizens accused of terrorism.

Much of Israel's success in fighting terrorism has been due to broad public support for Israel's antiterrorist policies. Israel's people have shown the will, and they have provided their government the resources, to fight terrorism. They entertain no illusions about the meaning or the danger of terrorism. Perhaps because they confront the threat every day, they recognize that they are at war with terrorism. The rest of us would do well to follow Israel's example.

But part of our problem here in the United States has been our seeming inability to understand terrorism clearly. Each successive terrorist incident has brought too much self-condemnation and dismay, accompanied by calls for a change in our policies or our principles or calls for withdrawal and retreat. We *should* be alarmed. We *should* be outraged. We *should* investigate and strive to improve. But widespread public anguish and self-condemnation only convince the terrorists that they are on the right track. It only encourages them to commit more acts of barbarism in the hope that American resolve will weaken.

This is a particular danger in the period before our election. If our reaction to terrorist acts is to turn on ourselves, instead of against the perpetrators, we give them redoubled incentive to do it again and to try to influence our political processes.

We have to be stronger, steadier, determined, and united in the face of the terrorist threat. We must not reward the terrorists by changing our policies or questioning our own principles or wallowing in self-flagellation or self-doubt. Instead, we should understand that terrorism is aggression and, like all aggression, must be forcefully resisted.

Requirements for an Active Strategy

We must reach a consensus in this country that our responses should go beyond passive defense to consider means of active prevention, pre-emption, and retaliation. Our goal must be to prevent and deter future terrorist acts, and experience has taught us over the years that one of the best deterrents to terrorism is the certainty that swift and sure measures will be taken against those who engage in it. We should take steps toward carrying out such measures. There should be no moral confusion on this issue. Our aim is not to seek revenge but to put an end to violent attacks against innocent people, to make the world a safer place to live for all of us. Clearly, the democracies have a moral right, indeed a duty, to defend themselves.

A successful strategy for combating terrorism will require us to face up to some hard questions and to come up with some clear-cut answers. The questions involve our intelligence capability, the doctrine under which we would employ force, and, most important of all, our public's attitude toward this challenge. Our nation cannot summon the will to act without firm public understanding and support.

First, our intelligence capabilities, particularly our human intelligence, are being strengthened. Determination and capacity to act are of little value unless we can come close to answering the questions: who, where, and when. We have to do a better job of finding out who the terrorists are; where they are; and the nature, composition, and patterns of behavior of terrorist organizations. Our intelligence services are organizing themselves to do the job, and they must be given the mandate and the flexibility to develop techniques of detection and contribute to deterrence and response.

Second, there is no question about our ability to use force where and when it is needed to counter terrorism. Our nation has forces prepared for action—from small teams able to operate virtually undetected to the full weight of our conventional military might. But serious issues are involved—questions that need to be debated, understood, and agreed if we are to be able to utilize our forces wisely and effectively.

If terrorists strike here at home, it is a matter for police action and domestic law enforcement. In most cases overseas, acts of terrorism against our people and installations can be dealt with best by the host government and its forces. It is worth remembering that just as it is the responsibility of the US government to provide security for foreign embassies in Washington, so the internationally agreed doctrine is that the security of our embassies abroad in the first instance is the duty of the host government, and we work with those governments cooperatively and with considerable success. The ultimate responsibility of course is ours, and we will carry it out with total determination and all the resources available to us. Congress, in a bipartisan effort, is giving us the legislative tools and the resources to strengthen the protection of our facilities and our people overseas—and they must continue to do so. But while we strengthen our defenses, defense alone is not enough.

The heart of the challenge lies in those cases where international rules and traditional practices do not apply. Terrorists will strike from areas where no governmental authority exists, or they will base themselves behind what they expect will be the sanctuary of an international border. And they will design their attacks to take place in precisely those gray areas where the full facts cannot be known, where the challenge will not bring with it an obvious or clear-cut choice of response.

In such cases we must use our intelligence resources carefully and completely. We will have to examine the full range of measures available to us to take. The outcome may be that we will face a choice between doing nothing or employing military force. We now recognize that terrorism is being used by our adversaries as a modern tool of warfare. It is no aberration. We can expect more terrorism directed at our strategic interests around the world in the years ahead. To combat it, we must be willing to use military force.

What will be required, however, is public understanding *before the fact* of the risks involved in combating terrorism with overt power:

- The public must understand *before the fact* that there is potential for loss of life of some of our fighting men and the loss of life of some innocent people.
- The public must understand *before the fact* that some will seek to cast any pre-emptive or retaliatory action by us in the worst light and will attempt to make our military and our policymakers—rather than the terrorists—appear to be the culprits.
- The public must understand *before the fact* that occasions will come when their government must act before each and every fact is known—and the decisions cannot be tied to the opinion polls.

Public support for US military actions to stop terrorists before they commit some hideous act or in retaliation for an attack on our people is crucial if we are to deal with this challenge.

Our military has the capability and the techniques to use power to fight the war against terrorism. This capability will be used judiciously.

To be successful over the long term, it will require solid support from the American people.

I can assure you that in this administration our actions will be governed by the rule of law; and the rule of law is congenial to action against terrorists. We will need the flexibility to respond to terrorist attacks in a variety of ways, at times and places of our own choosing. Clearly, we will not respond in the same manner to every terrorist act. Indeed, we will want to avoid engaging in a policy of automatic retaliation which might create a cycle of escalating violence beyond our control.

If we are going to respond or pre-empt effectively, our policies will have to have an element of unpredictability and surprise. And the prerequisite for such a policy must be a broad public consensus on the moral and strategic necessity of action. We will need the capability to act on a moment's notice. There will not be time for a renewed national debate after every terrorist attack. We may never have the kind of evidence that can stand up in an American court of law. But we cannot allow ourselves to become the Hamlet of nations, worrying endlessly over whether and how to respond. A great nation with global responsibilities cannot afford to be hamstrung by confusion and indecisiveness. Fighting terrorism will not be a clean or pleasant contest, but we have no choice but to play it.

We will also need a broader international effort. If terrorism is truly a threat to Western moral values, our morality must not paralyze us; it must give us the courage to face up to the threat. And if the enemies of these values are united, so, too, must the democratic countries be united in defending them. The leaders of the industrial democracies, meeting at the London summit in June, agreed in a joint declaration that they must redouble their cooperation against terrorism. There has been follow-up to that initial meeting, and the United States is committed to advance the process in every way possible. Since we, the democracies, are the most vulnerable, and our strategic interests are the most at stake, we must act together in the face of common dangers. For our part, we will work whenever possible in close cooperation with our friends in the democracies.

Sanctions, when exercised in concert with other nations, can help to isolate, weaken, or punish states that sponsor terrorism against us. Too often, countries are inhibited by fear of losing commercial opportunities or fear of provoking a bully. Economic sanctions and other forms of countervailing pressure impose costs and risks on the nations that apply them, but some sacrifices will be necessary if we are not to suffer even greater costs down the road. Some countries are clearly more vulnerable to extortion than others; surely this is an argument for banding together in mutual support, not an argument for appeasement.

If we truly believe in the values of our civilization, we have a duty to defend them. The democracies must have the self-confidence to tackle this menacing problem or else they will not be in much of a position to tackle other kinds of problems. If we are not willing to set limits to what kinds of behavior are tolerable, then our adversaries will conclude that there are no limits. As Thomas Jefferson once said, when we were confronted with the problem of piracy, "an insult unpunished is the parent of others." In a basic way, the democracies must show whether they believe in themselves.

We must confront the terrorist threat with the same resolve and determination that this nation has shown time and again throughout our history. There is no room for guilt or self-doubt about our right to defend a way of life that offers *all* nations hope for peace, progress, and human dignity. The sage Hillel expressed it well: "If I am not for myself, who will be? If I am for myself alone, who am I?"

As we fight this battle against terrorism, we must always keep in mind the values and way of life we are trying to protect. Clearly, we will not allow ourselves to descend to the level of barbarism that terrorism represents. We will not abandon our democratic traditions, our respect for individual rights, and freedom, for these are precisely what we are struggling to preserve and promote. Our values and our principles will give us the strength and the confidence to meet the great challenge posed by terrorism. If we show the courage and the will to protect our freedom and our way of life, we will prove ourselves again worthy of these blessings.

Originally published by the United States Department of State, Bureau of Public Affairs Office of Public Communication, Editorial Division, Washington, DC, October 1984, Editor: Colleen Sussman. This material is in the public domain and may be reproduced without permission; citation of this source is appreciated.

About the Author

GEORGE PRATT SHULTZ is the Thomas W. and Susan B. Ford Distinguished Fellow at the Hoover Institution. He attended Princeton University, graduating with a BA in economics, whereupon he enlisted in the US Marine Corps, serving through 1945. He later earned a PhD in industrial economics from the Massachusetts Institute of Technology. Shultz has had a distinguished career in government, in academia, and in the world of business. He is one of two individuals who have held four different federal cabinet posts; he has taught at three of this country's great universities; and for eight years he was president of a major engineering and construction company. Shultz was sworn in on July 16, 1982, as the sixtieth US secretary of state and served until January 20, 1989. In 1989, he was awarded the Presidential Medal of Freedom, the nation's highest civilian honor. His most recent book is *Issues on My Mind: Strategies for the Future* (Hoover Institution Press, 2013).

Index